10 Conversations

Also by Shmuley Boteach:

Dreams
The Wolf Shall Lie with the Lamb
Wrestling with the Divine
Wisdom, Understanding, and Knowledge
Moses of Oxford, Volumes I and II
Kosher Sex
Dating Secrets of the Ten Commandments
Kosher Emotions
The Rabbi and the Psychic
Why Can't I Fall in Love
Judaism for Everyone
The Private Adam
Kosher Adultery
Face Your Fear
Hating Women

10

CONVERSATIONS
YOU NEED TO
HAVE WITH YOUR
CHILDREN

❈ ❈ ❈ ❈ ❈ ❈ ❈ ❈ ❈ ❈

SHMULEY BOTEACH

wm

WILLIAM MORROW
An Imprint of HarperCollins*Publishers*

Designer: Publications Development Company of Texas

Library of Congress Cataloging-in-Publication Data has been applied for.

ISBN 13 978-0-06-113481-4

ISBN 10 0-06-113481-3

09   10   PDC/RRD   10   9   8   7

To my son Mendy,
on the occasion of your Bar Mitzvah.

May you grow to be a man who
uses words to inspire the world,
and change it for the better.

Contents

PROLOGUE

WHY CAN'T I GET MY CHILD TO LISTEN?
WHY DO I HAVE TO REPEAT EVERYTHING?
WHY DOES EVERY CONVERSATION
END IN AN ARGUMENT?

In my life as a family counselor—and on my family and parenting TV show, *Shalom in the Home*—I am approached constantly by parents looking for help with their children. It is a request I take very seriously; as a father of eight, I know how hard it can be to feel you've tried everything you can think of, to wonder whether you're being too indulgent or too harsh, too distant or too intrusive. Some parents are convinced that there's something wrong with them; others worry that there's something wrong with their kids. I remember one couple who joked, painfully, about their "devil daughter"—a child who opted to do wrong at every turn.

This book is based on two fundamental ideas. The first is that there are no bad children and no deliberately bad parents—but that sometimes, despite the best of intentions on both sides, there can be really bad relationships between parents and their children. The second is that, as parents, we must do everything we can to save those relationships, to reach out and communicate with our children. Because it is only by talking to them—really talking to them—that we can create an environment of inspiration and change.

That, then, is the purpose of this book: *to inspire parents to find creative ways to communicate with their increasingly uncommunicative kids.*

That is our fundamental job as parents—to take our children to the mountaintop; to become a source of knowledge, guidance, and inspiration; to help our children craft, shape, and mold their own characters—yet it remains the most neglected aspect of parenting. To the extent that we do speak to our kids at all, it's usually limited to set-piece conversations about the birds and the bees, say, or about the perils of drug abuse, and while those conversations are, of course, important, their limited repertoire would hardly constitute a real dialogue with our kids.

Parents always ask me, "Why can't I get my child to listen? Why do I have to repeat everything? Why does every conversation end in an argument?" And my answer is simple: "You are taking the wrong approach."

The job of the parent is not to impose his or her will on the child, but to get the child to *listen to his or her own inner voice*. Inspiration, not just prescription.

I can trace the idea for this book back to my long-ago days as a camp counselor, when I discovered that my principal function was to inspire the kids under my care. I soon realized that if I failed to find an outlet for their creative energies they would get into all sorts of mischief. Since I didn't want to spend my days playing traffic cop and peacekeeper, which is entirely reactionary and utterly lacking in inspiration, I tried to find creative ways to engage them. With a little work—challenging hikes, unusual games, unique adventures—I not only managed to keep them out of trouble, but to engage their minds, to make them come alive.

The Talmud says: *Idleness breeds sinfulness. When you have nothing to do, you do what you ought not to do.* Well, the Talmud is right.

That same approach can be applied to parenting. The parent who inspires his or her children is generally the most successful parent. But how does one inspire a child, especially in this day and age, when we hardly have enough time for ourselves? Inspiring people, lifting them up, is hard work, and it seems to require great storehouses of energy. Then again, perhaps it isn't as difficult as it appears. You might start by taking a closer look at yourself and your own values. When I did that, I had to come to terms with the fact that I was largely illiterate of the cultural arts, and that I would be unable to teach my children much about music, dance, opera, or ballet. On the other hand, there were many things I *did* know about, and I exposed my children to those: love of God, love of reading, love of history, love of nature, love of people, love of family. In sharing these passions with my kids, I may not have produced perfect children, but I can assure you that they don't lack for inspiration, and that they are rarely ever bored.

That alone has freed me from being a reactive parent, which seems to be the norm in most households these days. Your kid is drawing on the wall, you grab the crayons and stop him. Watching too much TV? You angrily turn off the set. Doesn't want to go bed? You raise your voice and send him running. Alas, that approach is fundamentally flawed. If you focus solely on crafting and shaping and molding your children, you will raise kids who are trying to become what they think Mom and Dad want them to become, not what they themselves would like to be. Or, worse, you'll raise angry young rebels. But if you stop being so reactionary, and if you take the time to be proactive, you can teach the child to find his own way, and to listen to his own, unique, inner voice.

That is the purpose of these *10 Conversations:* to help you put your child in touch with his own heart so that he will be prepared for the all-important questions: *What kind of person do I want to be? Do I want to be a good person or a bad person? Do I want to be selfless or selfish? Will I bring light into the world, or will I compound its darkness? Will I live life in the shallows, or will I engage its mysteries and plumb its depths?*

In a phrase, these conversations are about *becoming a person.*

In the book of Psalms (127), David describes the parent as a quiver and the child as an arrow. Long after the arrow has left the bow, its trajectory is shaped by the bow. Have you imparted to your child the inspiration that will have him traveling along a righteous path? Have you given your child the tools he needs to face the world? Are you fulfilling your role as a source of guidance and inspiration? Are your kids turning into the kinds of kids you hoped they would become?

When people meet my kids, they always tell me how nice they are, but my kids are not nice in a boring, goody-two-shoes sense. They argue, fight among themselves, and sometimes get reprimanded by teachers for not working hard enough at school. On the other hand, they do have a certain maturity that many kids lack, and this is what people notice about them. When we have large groups of guests for dinner, which we do almost every Friday night for the Jewish Sabbath, my kids will sit at the table and actively engage the adults in conversation. They do so because they are genuinely interested in hearing what people have to say and have already, at an early age, formed strong opinions on a plethora of subjects, and I'd like to think that my wife and I had a little something to do with this. We have tried to teach our children to be curious about people and about life, to ask questions, to probe deeper. In short, we have tried to inspire in them a hunger for living—for the sheer mystery of being alive. And we've done this by talking to our kids, *really* talking to them.

Indeed, if my kids do something wrong, rather than just getting upset about it—which I do from time to time—I have trained myself to see it as an opportunity to initiate a conversation. Sure, bad behavior invites punishment and discipline. But it also calls for an attempt to inspire.

That, then, is the focus of these *10 Conversations:* to help you, the parent, learn to communicate effectively with your child; to light the way; to be a beacon of inspiration; to *really* talk to them. As you read this book, and allow yourself to be influenced by it, I will ask you to recognize that every experience has the potential to be turned into a conversation starter, that every experience can be distilled into gold—if you simply condition yourself to see it. Whenever something happens in the course of my day, no matter how insignificant it might appear, I always look for that special moment: "There it is! That's the beginning of this evening's conversation!"

These *10 Conversations* are not just "seminal ideas" for conversations, but a guide designed to steer you toward a wholly new way of parenting. It is my firm belief that this book will help you become a more effective parent, and that in so doing you will raise children who will always reach for the highest plane.

The Talmud says: *Words that emanate from the heart, penetrate the heart.*

Brace yourself for wonderful changes!

10 Conversations

1

On Becoming a Person

The question becomes,
"Who, not what, do you want to be?"

We are all born with a desire to be good—I firmly believe this—but it can be very challenging to be good *all the time*. This is particularly so for children, who are relatively new to the whole concept of goodness, and who need all the help they can get as they struggle to define it.

In our home, there is one question that is heard on almost a daily basis: *Who do you want to be?* The choice speaks to character, not career, and the issue is the same for all of us: *Do you want to be a good person, or do you want to be a bad person?*

Compared to this, every other choice in life is small potatoes. Your child could become president of the United States, he could become the wealthiest, most successful industrialist on the planet, but if he is a bad person you will have failed as a parent. And that's the power of this conversation: You need to teach your child that every choice in life is subordinate to the moral choice.

∽

EVERY CHOICE IN LIFE IS SUBORDINATE TO THE MORAL CHOICE.

∽

Let me give you an example of how we do this at our home. One night, not long ago, I was on my way to speak at *Shalva*, an organization that helps parents with handicapped children. They were holding a fund-raiser in Long Island, and I was donating my time as a guest speaker because I really believe in the organization. Families are often torn asunder when they have a handicapped child, and *Shalva* tries to save both the child and the marriage.

I was being taken out to Long Island by a driver, a fine man I'd met two or three times before, and I was sitting in back, reviewing my speech, when my cell phone rang. It was my second daughter, Chana, asking if I had time for her. I always try to make time for my kids, even when I don't have time, so I told her I had a minute or two. She plunged right in: "I spoke to Mommy, and Mommy said it's okay already. I want to dye my hair a bit of a darker shade of brown. It's not permanent, but I want to try it out." And I said, "Well, Chana, let's talk about this when I get home. I'm on my way to a charity event at the moment, and I'm trying to polish my speech." And Chana said, quite forcefully, "*No, Tatty*. Please give me an answer. Mommy said it was okay. It's not permanent."

I was distracted, and I repeated that I didn't want to get into it, telling Chana we would talk later. Not an hour later, while I was sitting at the fund-raiser, in the middle of dinner, my cell phone rang. It was Chana again, pressing me for an answer, and I was so irritated that I took the easy way out and relented. "Fine," I said. "If you're going to push me, and if it really isn't permanent and no big deal, go ahead and do it!"

A couple of hours later, when I was on the way home, it occurred to me that the driver must be hungry. He had waited outside in the car while I'd been inside the estate of a Long Island billionaire, enjoying a seven-course meal. When we finally pulled up to my home, I asked the driver if he wanted to come in for a bite to eat. At first he refused, politely, but he finally relented, admitting that he really was quite hungry, and I brought him into the house.

I found Chana at the computer, working on her homework, studying for a big test, and I asked her to go into the kitchen and prepare a little something for the driver. She heated up dinner, made him a nice salad, and waited on him. And after the driver had gone home, no longer hungry, I turned to her and told her that her hair looked nice. "You really like it?" she asked.

"Yes," I said. "It's a beautiful shade of brown, although I still prefer your natural color. But there's something more important I want to talk to you about." I indicated the chair in front of me, and we sat facing each other. "Let me tell you a story about two girls. The first girl is prepared to call her father and bug him over something superficial, shallow, and self-serving, even after she's been told that he is busy preparing for an important charity event. The other girl is at home, in front of her computer, studying for an important test, but when her father asks her to prepare dinner for a hungry stranger, she does it willingly and without complaint. This second girl treats the guest as if he were a visiting dignitary, and when her father sees this he is filled with pride. It is a story of two different girls, Chana. One girl, really, but with two totally different facets. Who do you think I'm talking about?"

And she smiled a little and said, "Me?"

"That's right," I said. "You have to choose, Chana. One cancels the other out. The two girls inside you will forever battle for predominance, and you have to choose: *Which one of those girls do you want to be?*"

The fact is, I *know* she wants to be the good girl, and that's not just a matter of opinion. *All* children want to be good. From time immemorial, civilization has focused much of its energy on preserving the innocence of the child—the innocence that is his birthright. Then Sigmund Freud came along, and everything he said about human development undermined the very notion of childhood innocence. Children were narcissistic and uncivilized, he suggested. They were sexual from birth. They had to be *controlled.* As these notions became more and more accepted in modern society, people stopped seeing children as good and innocent. Suddenly they were bent on purging their children of all of these unseemly qualities, and protecting them from corrosive, external influences. But nothing could be more absurd! Children are neither good nor bad.

> ☙
>
> CHILDREN ARE A BLANK SLATE ON WHICH WE PARENTS WILL DO OUR WRITING.
>
> ☙

They are a blank slate on which we parents will do our writing.

Let me tell you another story about this all-important question—*Do I want to be a good person or a bad person?*—this one involving my eldest daughter, Mushki. My wife Debbie is from Australia, and her parents still live there, and they don't get to see their grandchildren very often. As a result, there's a certain feeling of woundedness. They know our kids are closer to my own parents, who live here, in the United States, but that closeness is a result of geography, nothing else. Whenever they come to visit, however, about every two years, there's an initial sense of alienation and distance, and I can see it is very painful for them, and I feel it in my heart. Now, I love my mother-in-law, but she is the only child of Holocaust survivors, and she tends to be a little overprotective. I can understand the reasons for it, but my wife and I have worked hard at not being overprotective parents, and our kids have strong personalities and value their (relative) independence.

One morning, my mother-in-law went into Mushki's room and asked her to do something. Mushki found the idea a bit babyish, and they got into an argument. My mother-in-law came downstairs in tears, and it was clear that she and Mushki had had words. In our household, this is unacceptable. Our kids have been taught to respect their elders, and to respect their grandparents in particular. There are no exceptions to this rule. I could have stormed upstairs and confronted Mushki—"Don't ever again speak to your grandmother disrespectfully! Apologize to her at once!" But I didn't do that. For me, it wasn't simply disrespect, but an act of insensitivity, and I wanted my daughter to understand how she had hurt her grandmother.

I called Mushki downstairs and took her into the dining room. "Look," I said, "your grandmother is crying over this argument, and I want you to understand something: This goes beyond respect for your elders. This is a woman who loves you and lives very far away, and she feels this great distance between you, both geographic and emotional. And you are her first grandchild. You made her a grandmother. So when she comes here and asks you to do something, and you find it a bit babyish, do it anyway. Humor her. Being a good person is not a choice we make when it's convenient. It's a choice we make even when we feel uncomfortable, or slightly degraded, by the moral choice."

My daughter said nothing, so I pressed on: "Who do you want to be, Mushki? Do you want to be the kind of person who is always healing a heart, who is always mending the wounds of a broken heart, or do you want to be someone who fragments a human heart? You choose. You can be one or the other, but you can't be both. Which will it be?"

I could have approached our talk somewhat differently. I could have simply asked my daughter to apologize to her grandmother, which is the common approach, but I don't think that makes for adequate parenting. That approach would have made her a passive listener. She would have obeyed, and we would have been done with it, but she would have learned nothing. Children know right from wrong. They have an innate sense of justice. What you hear from them most often is, "That's not fair! She got a bigger piece of chocolate!" Or, "His present cost more!" Parents need to listen to that. Kids *know* the difference. They instinctively feel when something is fair, and when it's unfair. And if they don't know it, you must help them figure it out for themselves. Telling a child how to behave is not nearly as effective as inspiring him with a sense of what he wants to be. Not *do*, but *be*. A child who is asked to think about the type of person he wants to be will begin changing on his own, without nagging and prodding. But you have to *inspire* him to do so.

A CHILD WHO IS ASKED TO THINK ABOUT THE TYPE OF PERSON HE WANTS TO BE WILL BEGIN CHANGING ON HIS OWN, WITHOUT NAGGING AND PRODDING. BUT YOU HAVE TO INSPIRE HIM TO DO SO.

I tried this approach with one of the families that I met through my TV show, a divorced mother and her four children. The mother was completely broken by housework, aged well beyond her years by sadness and frustration, and the children did absolutely nothing to help her. I took the oldest child aside, Claire, a girl of sixteen, and engaged her in conversation. I could have told her that she was being narcissistic and selfish, and lambasted her for being a spoiled brat, but that would only have made her defensive. And even if that had somehow motivated her to begin helping around the house, she would have been doing so out of guilt, not inspiration. For me, this never works: Guilt is a terrible and unreliable motivator. It gets us to do things, but we do them without joy.

Instead, I prodded her to listen to her own inner voice, and began by asking her to describe the most painful experience of her life. She didn't even have to think about it. It was her parents' divorce, she said, and its painful aftermath. "My father is never around," she told me. "He doesn't care about me at all."

"Do you want to be like your father?" I asked her.

"Never," she said. "He only cares about himself. He's not a good person."

"So you want to be different? You want to be a good person?"

"Definitely," she answered.

"Do you want to be a good person more than anything else in the entire world?"

"Yes," she said.

"Well, let me ask you this: Does a good person treat her mother like a cleaning woman?"

That conversation actually turned things around for Claire. She had been reprimanded, tirelessly, for not helping out, but she had never seen her behavior in terms of goodness. And since she wanted to be a good person, and wanted to see herself as a good person, she began to change.

Goodness is its own reward, but it has practical applications, too. Often, for example, I will walk into one of my kids' rooms, and the room is sloppy, and I will sit him or her down and say, "You live in this house. You sleep in this room. This is your room, your private space. Do you want to live in squalor? Do you want to grow accustomed to living in a mess?" I try to impress on them that this is a representation of who they are. People *do* judge a book by its cover, and when a person walks into a messy room, they see someone who is disorganized and lazy. So I ask my kids: *Is this who you want to be?*

"Do you want to be the kind of person who is ashamed to bring friends home because his room is unkempt? Or do you want to be the kind of person who values and respects his property, but who is lazy about such things?"

Indolence is a big issue with kids. I talk to my kids about it all the time. "To be alive is to be *fully* alive," I tell them. "And you have to force yourself to do things you don't want to do. One of the keys to living a good life is self-motivation. Throughout life, always search for people and places that inspire you so that you are motivated to develop your fullest potential."

I often look for examples to illustrate my points. I have talked to my kids about the Kabbalah, the mystical branch of Judaism, to help them distinguish between *external will* and *internal will*. The difference is really quite simple. To paraphrase a song the Spice Girls sang, it boils down to making a distinction between what we want, and what we *really, really want*. External will is what we want as a result of social pressure. Internal will is what we want as individuals, regardless of any kind of external influence. And this, too, speaks directly to the notion of who we want to be. Do we want to respond to outside influences, or do we want to develop our own, inner voice?

Let me give you an example: You take your kid to a restaurant and he begins ladling soup onto his head. People turn to watch, and you are mortified by this animal you've raised, so you yell at him, "Stop that right now!" The child stops, but the only reason he does so is because you've frightened him into it. He hasn't internalized that message. He has only stopped because the policeman is at the table, and when you leave the table he will probably do it again. He hasn't learned any manners, he has only learned to respond to your anger. That's external will, and it teaches him nothing.

Ironically, the child understands, almost intuitively, that you don't care whether he puts soup in his hair. It's not something you ever really talked about. And you're only reacting this time because there are people around and you are ashamed of his table manners. You reprimand him not because you care about *him*, but because you care about the neighbors. Well, he senses this, too. Someone else is looking, and that forces you to do something about it. But I repeat: This is not internal will; it is external will. And it works, certainly. You always get immediate results from external will. But it never lasts because the child is not being taught to internalize it. The child is not being attuned to his own inner voice.

That voice goes by many names—*Conscience, Soul, Spirit, Innermost Will, Deepest Self*—but it all means the same thing: It is the very core of our being, our *essence*, the point at which we can't delve any deeper. I can't tell you what's down in your inner soul, and even if I knew I'm not sure I could put it into words, but I know it speaks, in part, to our humanity and our goodness. And don't kid yourself: Children know all about goodness. When they hurt someone, they know to regret it; when they make their parents lives difficult, they know to feel lousy; when they treat a person with disrespect, they are remorseful to the core of their being. The problems begin if the child is allowed to behave in contradiction to his deepest self, because he becomes progressively more alienated from the forces of good, and in time they will no longer have any influence on him. Real, effective parenting—which is also the most humane form of parenting—is all about *helping the child reconnect with his essence, all about putting him in touch with his innermost self.*

That inner voice needs to be an integral part of a child's life, *always*. Rules are fine, but they don't address character, and in the long term they add up to very little. The parent who wants the best for his child will always think about internal will. He is not looking for quick fixes. That parent will not yell when the child puts soup in his hair. Instead, he will get him to stop, and then he will communicate. "You know, Brian, I'm your father and I love you, so let me ask you a simple question: In life, what do you think is the main thing that distinguishes human beings from animals?"

He might venture a guess: "Intelligence?"

"No," you reply. "Animals think. They may not think in the same way we think, but they employ intelligence, which has been demonstrated in many different ways. What distinguishes us from animals is that we have dignity. We put on clothing, for example, because we want to protect our human dignity. Animals don't care; they go around naked. We eat with a knife and a fork; animals just stick their head in a trough. Human beings behave in a dignified, *human* manner, and that's what separates us from animals. I want you to respect yourself. A gentleman eats with a fork and knife. And he's careful. And if he spills food, he wipes it up. And he doesn't burp at the table. And he always, always eats in a refined manner."

Now, admittedly, a conversation like that is not always going to make an impact, and at first it might even appear less effective than yelling. The child might be sullen, unresponsive, dismissive even: "Yeah! Whatever!" But when you have that same conversation two or three more times, you will start getting through to him. That's internal will. No one is coercing you, the parent, to have this talk with him. No external pressure is being brought to bear on you. You are doing it from the heart, because you really care about him, not because you're worried about being embarrassed. And he's going to *feel* that. As I said earlier, *words that emanate from the heart, penetrate the heart.* Little by little, your words will break though his resistance.

This is what we call *the long, shorter way.* External will is the short, longer way. You yell at the kid and you get an immediate result: He stops ladling soup onto his head. But he learns nothing, and it will be a long time before he internalizes any manners.

Internal will is the long, shorter way. What exactly is the long, shorter way? Let me illustrate. According to a story in the Talmud, one day a man was traveling to a city, and he came to a fork in the road. He didn't know the best way to the city, and he saw a young boy standing at the fork so he asked him, "How do I get to the city?" The boy said, "Well, it depends. Do you want the long, shorter way or the short, longer way?" Now, the average person who hears that question would want the short, longer way—you want what's easiest first, right? So the man said he wanted the short, longer way, and the boy pointed him in the right direction. The short, longer way took the man straight to the city, but not to one of the city gates. He tried to find his way to the gates, but he got lost, and he even tried to scale the walls. When he couldn't manage it, he returned to the fork in the road, frustrated, and again addressed the boy. "Didn't you say this path was shorter?" he asked. And the boy responded, "And didn't I also say that it was *longer*?" The boy pointed him in a different direction this time, the long, shorter way, which was somewhat more roundabout, and did indeed take longer, but it led the man straight to the gate.

The moral of the story is simple: If you're looking for immediate glory, you may well find it—but it is unlikely to last. The easy choice is seldom the right choice. The point is this: It is easier to yell at your child—"Do this now!"—but he won't internalize anything. "Oh, Dad's in a bad mood," he'll think. "He must have had a lousy day at the office." If this teaches him anything, it will teach him not to ladle soup onto his head when you're around. But it will be a long time before he learns to stop doing so on his own. In his eyes, you are a police officer, and he will watch himself when you are present. But that does absolutely nothing for him. He has learned nothing.

On the other hand, if you converse with him, if you take the long, shorter way, he will find his own voice. It's hard work, and it will doubtless take longer, but it is in fact the shorter way. The child who listens to his own, inner voice, the child who learns to think about *who he wants to be*, will make your task as a parent a great deal easier.

As you put this into practice, there is one important element you mustn't lose sight of: Children, like adults, soon tire of having their flaws pointed out to them. Constant criticism results not from your desire to help your child, but from your inability to deal with pressure. The goal is to inspire our children, not berate them. Admonishing must be done sparingly to have any effect, and must not be overdone. Give your children a break from time to time, but never stop nourishing that inner voice. Open their eyes to the world around them. Make them truly *see*. And look for opportunities to do so.

I'm a marital counselor, and I hear incredibly heartbreaking stories every week. Sometimes, at dinner, I tell my children some of these stories, without of course naming names or betraying confidences. Recently, I told them this story: "A middle-aged couple came to see me, and the marriage was suffering because the husband was hypercritical. He criticized everything his wife did—the way a lot of men do, unfortunately. These men are miserable on the inside, so they treat their wives miserably on the outside. And the wife couldn't find it in her heart to show her husband any affection. As it happened, he had arranged a family trip to Cincinnati, to see his parents, and she didn't want to go. She wanted to show him: *You can't treat me badly.* So she called me and told me that she wasn't going to go to Cincinnati with her husband, and I knew that this would only exacerbate the problems in the marriage." I stopped and looked around the table at my children, all of whom were listening attentively. "Well?" I asked. "What do you think she should do?"

There was an immediate outcry: "She shouldn't go!" "He's not nice to her." "Stay home and teach him a lesson!" "Dump him!"

"No," I said to my kids. "You're all wrong. Don't you get it? You can never go wrong when you do the right thing. The husband wanted to take his wife and his children to see his parents. And I advised her to go. I said, 'The right thing is to go to Cincinnati, and to show his parents respect. Even if the marriage is bad, they're still the grandparents and the grandkids have to learn to show them respect. So even if you're in pain, you go, and you show his parents respect. Don't you see? Your husband's whole problem is that he doesn't know how to show respect. You need to be an example to him by doing the right thing.

> ❦
>
> YOU CAN NEVER GO WRONG WHEN YOU DO THE RIGHT THING.
>
> ❦

You need to go because it's the right thing to do, and *you can never go wrong when you do the right thing*. You're not being a doormat by showing respect to two elderly people. Rather, you're being a good person. This isn't about your husband. It's about doing the right thing. And if the marriage ends up collapsing, at least you did the right thing, and that is its own reward. You never compromised your own morality.'"

When I talk to my kids about such things, I am simply talking to them, in a roundabout way, about *who they want to be*. How they must strive to do the right thing in all circumstances. These conversations become a guide to life. Children know that marriages fail, that people can be cruel and abusive, that the road ahead is not always smooth. So why not inspire them with a commitment to righteousness amid the trials of life? What better way to prepare them?

I tell my kids, "Marriages fall apart because people don't listen to their own voices. They become reactive, victims of external will. 'My husband is mean to me! I should be mean back!' No. That's wrong. You always have to do the right thing. And how do you know what the right thing is? You know, because you listen to your inner voice of conscience. We always know when we are betraying ourselves. The problem, when we do wrong, is not that we've lost our inner moral compass, but that we've generated enough noise to drown it out. We may not want to hear it, but we *know*. And it is especially important to do the right thing in times of crises. That's what I tell the couples who come to see me, because doing the right thing is what keeps marriages together. If both the husband and the wife always did the right thing, they would stop hurting each other. The decision to do the right thing is paramount. It's the most important thing."

When your child begins to understand this, it puts his entire life into a moral context: *We do the right thing because it's right.* Not because God is watching, although He *is* watching, but because we have an inner Godliness, an inner voice that knows right from wrong. And we *want* to do the right thing, just as we want people to know that we've done the right thing.

This was something Dale Carnegie understood, and it resulted in one of the most successful books of the twentieth century: *How to Win Friends and Influence People.* He knew that everybody's deepest desire was to be good, and that the deepest insult was to tell someone they were bad. In his book, Carnegie argued that a key way to ingratiate yourself with others was to let them know that you thought they were good. Handsome, successful, charming—certainly, but above all they wanted to hear that they were *good.*

We all want to be seen as good people, he said, which is why we go to such great lengths to protect our good names.

Senator John McCain is an example. He spent five years as a prisoner-of-war in Vietnam, and it was certainly terribly painful, but he said it was nothing compared to the pain he felt when he was accused of being part of the Keating Five. He was absolutely crushed by the notion that people would think he was a corrupt politician, and that he had used his power to grant favors to a savings and loan magnate. He didn't want to be thought of as a *bad* person.

Thomas Jefferson is another example. He endured more than his share of pain in his life, losing his wife and several children over the years, but when he was governor of Virginia during the Revolutionary War, and found himself forced to flee the British, he was accused of cowardice. Years later, he said that the pain on that occasion was almost unbearable—worse than anything he had ever experienced. The idea that people thought he had betrayed the revolutionary struggle, that he wasn't a *good* person, was apparently more painful than the death of his wife and children. People not only want to be good, they want to be *thought of* as good, which is why they go to such lengths to clear their names and protect their reputations.

When a parent talks to his child about his behavior, and about the behavior of people in the world around him, and even about the behavior of historical figures, he is reinforcing the child's innate sense of goodness, inspiring him to embrace the righteous. *This is how people behave. Some people behave well. Some people behave badly. How are you going to behave? Who and what do you want to be?*

If you are constantly telling your child what to do, he will resist and argue and even defy you, and your job as a parent will become increasingly exhausting. But if you work on motivating your child to hear that inner voice, the voice of conscience, you will inspire him to become a better person. There is simply no greater motivator than to have a child develop a commitment to himself, to who he wants to be, rather than to his parents, who are telling him what he should be. When misbehaving, a child should never be made to feel as if he has betrayed his parents or his teachers; *it is much more effective if he feels he has betrayed himself.*

That is why we ask the question, and why we must never stop asking it: *Who do you want to be?*

2

CHILDHOOD AND HAPPINESS

A PERSON WHO WAS TRULY A CHILD FIRST,
A PERSON WHO EXPERIENCED LIFE AS
SOMETHING WONDERFUL AND AWE-INSPIRING,
TAKES THAT WITH HIM INTO ADULTHOOD.

I often talk to my kids about my father, whom I love very much but with whom I have always had a complicated relationship. After my parents' divorce, when I was eight years old, my mother moved us from Los Angeles to Miami, where my grandparents lived. We seldom saw my father—never more than a few times a year—and his absence scarred me deeply.

It has always been difficult for my father to show emotion. He was born into extreme poverty in Iran and had to struggle his entire life, against great odds, to succeed. I do not judge my father. I consider him a great man, filled with determination, charisma, vision, and an iron commitment to Jewish tradition. In many ways, he's the proudest man I know. I'm honored to be his son, but his external toughness has often made it difficult for us to be close.

My kids love their grandfather, and consider him the most unique and colorful man in the world. They see him as a Middle Eastern version of Indiana Jones. They're mesmerized by him, and they want to be closer to him. But they find roadblocks in the way. My father's difficult life has affected him deeply. He has a generous and loving heart, but on the outside he is tough and leathery.

I say to my kids, "You see how Saba has allowed life to get to him? Even when he was a child, he couldn't be a child. He had to help support his thirteen brothers and sisters from when he was age ten. So because he couldn't be a child, he lost his inner child. Now he lets everything get to him; even little things sap his spirit.

"That's one of the reasons it's such a challenge to get close to him. You're children, and he never enjoyed any inner youthfulness—he had to steel himself against the world—so he finds it difficult to relate to you. From the time he was a boy, he had to be a man, and through no fault of his own Saba has allowed his inner child to dissipate. He has never learned to be a child. So that's your job now as his grandchildren. You have to play with him and teach him how it's done. You have to bring out his lost inner youthfulness."

When I speak to my children about this, I am trying to impress upon them that childhood isn't just a transient phase—that it isn't meant to be ephemeral. This is a critical phase in life, one that you're supposed to internalize and carry with you into the future.

I believe that some of the most successful men and women are those who have stayed in touch with their inner child. Steven Spielberg and George Lucas are two examples: They are successful adults, certainly, but they also know how to communicate with children—because in many ways they are still children themselves. They are unashamedly playful and revel in their childlike imagination. Albert Einstein was another, with his tousled hair and his utter disregard for adult conventions. So was Richard Feynman, the celebrated American physicist who loved nothing more than a good practical joke. Michelangelo, Picasso, Mozart, Brahms, Beethoven—all of these men were famous for their childlike nature. They were playful, curious, imaginative, creative, and endlessly energetic. In short, they were kids in adult bodies.

"When you grow up, I want you to be responsible, mature adults," I tell my children. "But I want you to have a child at your center. Whatever heartbreak you might one day experience as an adult, you should remain a child on the inside because a child is resilient, a child always bounces back.

"Remember the story in the Bible about the cherubim—the baby-faced angels that God placed at the gates to the Garden of Eden after he evicted Adam and Eve? God put them there to protect the Garden, and the meaning of the story couldn't be clearer: If you cultivate and nourish the child inside you, that child will always lead you back to Paradise.

"The Garden of Eden was not only a place in space, it was above all a place in *time*. It represents our childhood years, when everything is magical and perfect. Eviction from the Garden represents growing up, and when you grow up you will face your share of hardship and disappointment. But if that child remains alive inside you, you will always have Eden on the inside. You'll never give up hope because you've been to Paradise and can revisit it as often as you like."

I genuinely believe that. I believe that all of us carry our childhood with us into the future, and that we can tap into our inner child at any moment because that child is always with us—internalized and eternalized. To me, the perfect person is the man or woman who has managed to fuse the child with the adult. The virtues of being an adult are many: You're responsible, you're capable, you're strong, you learn a little something from the vicissitudes of life, you gain wisdom from experience. But the shortcomings are plentiful, too: in the process of becoming an adult, you've been hurt, you're more cynical, you're scarred, you're not as sensitive, you're not as tender, you're less trusting, you're more ambitious and aggressive, and—perhaps most tragic—you find out that people aren't always as kind and good as you had hoped, and you tend to lose interest in "playing with others."

The inner child can protect you from this. Children *love* to play with others. They hate being alone. They love sharing, openness, tenderness, novelty. They are curious about life. They haven't been diminished by setbacks. A young child is not self-conscious about being needy, or about showing his parents and his friends that he wants love. They're not perfect, of course. Children can be immature and cranky and irresponsible and undisciplined. But they are open to life. And that's critical, because as the years take their toll, we become more removed and distant, more alone.

This is why your children must live fully as children. A person who was truly a child first, a person who experienced life as something wonderful and awe-inspiring, takes that with him into adulthood. He permanently internalizes the magic and sense of wonder and that gives him the best of both worlds: the strength, seriousness, and emerging wisdom of adulthood, with the boundless joy of the child within. That is what Adam and Eve were all about: Their childlike and adult qualities had been perfectly amalgamated. And that is what we need to strive for. An adult who is able to internalize his inner child remains creative, youthful, and joyful well into his later years. An adult without an inner child, on the other hand, is like a house with a rickety foundation—forever in danger of toppling over.

"Don't be in such a hurry to grow up," I tell my kids. "In life there are two paths: One, to focus always on the destination, to live with anxiety and nervousness, always worried about when you're going to get there. The person who focuses on his destination never derives any real satisfaction from his achievements because he always lives in permanent anticipation. He is always waiting for the next big thing, so he doesn't enjoy the journey, and when he reaches his goal he feels empty because the race is over. He must now set for himself yet another goal, which—once attained—will likewise fail to provide him with a sense of satisfaction.

"The other path, the wiser and nobler one, is to focus on the journey. To enjoy the road with all its scenery; to be *means*-oriented as opposed to *goal*-oriented. A good life is measured by the distance we have traveled, not by the mountains we have climbed. The means-oriented man really enjoys the journey. He's not worried about where it's going to lead. He's not wearing blinders, not focused on the goal alone, but is open to the world around him. His life is filled with beauty and wonder, and he learns to enjoy it fully."

It is very important to communicate this to your kids, to teach them to be *in the moment*. One of the reasons so many adults are so empty is because they never learned this. They don't know how to enjoy the present. They live and die with dreams, and—being immersed in dreams—are never sufficiently awake to enjoy reality. They want to achieve this or that by such and such an age. The locus of their happiness is always *outside* of them. "If I get to be a vice president by this age, I'll be happy." "If I can afford that big house, my dream will have been realized and I will be a happy man."

But they aren't happy. Not really. The job will never be good enough; there's a better job on the floor upstairs. The house will never be large enough; look at that double lot at the end of the block. When the future arrives, it is always less than they expected. And still they don't learn!

A young child, on the other hand, a *very young* child, approaches the world in a markedly different manner. A young child doesn't think ahead. He enjoys the moment. He isn't interested in any goals beyond the immediate ones. Even the smallest things, like bringing a blank piece of paper to life with color, can be deeply satisfying to the child, because that is all there is for him: that precious, present moment. And that's part of the conversation I have with my children: I try to cultivate and nourish the child's natural tendency to stay in the moment without anticipating an ulterior end. A child who learns to live in the now becomes a better adjusted adult.

Unfortunately, as children approach their teens, they seem to become ever more eager to leave childhood behind, and this adolescent hunger for adulthood becomes especially pronounced when there are problems in the home. "I can't wait till I'm eighteen!" the child will say after an argument with his parents. "I'll finally get away from this crazy house!" These kids are often reacting to what they perceive as criticism—*Your room is a mess. Your grades need to improve. You left your chores undone*—and getting out of the house represents freedom. But they need to understand that true freedom comes from within.

The key is *to educate and inspire without lecturing*. When I talk to my kids about the more delicate matters, I often use examples from my own experiences. I tell them, "I have made mistakes in my life, which I regret deeply, but in virtually every circumstance, when I made those mistakes, it was due to my inability to hear criticism from someone else, notably parents, teachers, and friends. I was weak; I wasn't robust enough on the inside to take criticism on the outside. If you take a straw man and give him a slight push, he falls apart. But the strong man takes criticism, and in fact seeks it out. The weak man can't listen to any advice or guidance. He feels wounded by even the slightest criticism. Anywhere you touch him, he is injured—that's how fragile he is. And that's what led to some of my greatest mistakes: my own fragility. The strong man or strong woman is malleable, because even when they are bent by criticism, they are not bent out of shape. They have an inner core."

And part of that inner core is the *inner voice*—the child's innate desire to be good. As a parent, you need to nourish that child, and hope that your child will remain receptive enough, for long enough, to let you do your job properly. If you tear a young tree out of the ground when its roots are still weak, it might survive, but will it thrive?

There are some topics that have absolutely no place in the life of a child. Marital conflicts, for example. Finances. Sex. These are taboo in my home, and that's by design. What do I mean by this? I mean that if you inspire your kids, if you've transformed them through genuine conversation, those aren't going to be issues. A kid who listens to his inner voice of conscience isn't going to need to listen to a one-sided conversation about drugs: *He already knows better.* A teenage girl whose parents have instilled within her a strong sense of dignity, confidence, and a commitment to goodness thinks way too much of love to even consider cheapening it through anonymous sex. When you teach your child to hear his inner voice, you stop being a police officer, which is the least enjoyable part of parenting—and the most distancing. It makes for unhappy parents and unhappy children, and unhappy children tend to want to rush into adulthood.

Everyone is unhappy from time to time, of course, even children, but I see happiness as a choice. The problem is that we tend *to find reasons to be unhappy.* I do it, too. "My last book sold pretty well, but it didn't reach the top of the bestseller list! Woe is me!"

Sometimes I'll talk to my kids about my own shortcomings to illustrate a point. My second daughter Chana, for example, inherited a more serious, sometimes even melancholic side, from me, and in our frequent talks I try to inspire her to choose joy.

"Many people believe that happiness is the organic outcome of a happy disposition, or that happiness depends on what happens on any given day," I tell her. "You get good news, you're happy. You get bad news, you're sad. And it shows: When you're happy, you smile. When you're sad, you mope. But this is backward. Happiness is a choice. If you act happy, you will feel happy. The emotions do not dictate your actions; your actions dictate your emotions."

This is one of life's most important lessons, and one of the most critical things we need to teach our children. The conventional thinking is that how we feel on the inside dictates how we behave on the outside. This would make us slaves to our emotions and guarantee a life that is often out of our control. But the truth is precisely the opposite. When we force ourselves to behave in a certain way, even if we don't feel it, the action creates the emotion. When you force yourself to treat people lovingly, for example, you slowly begin to care for them, even if you didn't much care for them at first.

> ONE OF THE GREAT SECRETS OF LIFE IS THAT YOU CAN CONTROL YOUR EMOTIONS BY CONTROLLING YOUR ACTIONS.

Conversely, if you ignore the people you love, and rarely show affection, that love will wither and dissipate over time. I have witnessed as much in far too many marriages.

I tell my children, "If you treat someone lovingly, even if you feel no real compassion for them, even if you feel *contempt* for them, you are practicing kindness, and you will begin to *feel* kindness.

"You can't always wait around for happy emotions to come flooding along, because you could be waiting a very long time. One of the great secrets of life is that you can control your emotions by controlling your actions."

In other words, when we're unhappy, we are choosing to be unhappy. We are choosing to reflect on things that make us unhappy. We are choosing to focus on the pessimistic outlook. Conversely, when we choose joy, we are consciously choosing to dismiss those things that make us unhappy. On close inspection, we see that they are petty and insubstantial. When we dismiss the feelings, we are choosing joy, and joy above all other emotions keeps us young.

Most people expect happiness to come washing over them like a wave, and this certainly happens from time to time. But more often than not, happiness is a conscious choice. We can choose to focus on the things that bring us down, or we can choose to focus on our blessings. After all, as the great German thinker Immanuel Kant himself noted: "It is not God's will merely that we should be happy, but that we should make ourselves happy."

Certainly, there are times when we are unable to shake our feelings of unhappiness, and I myself have often struggled with that type of free-floating unhappiness. I would become inexplicably despondent and couldn't even make the effort to fight it.

I say to my children all the time: "I want you to learn from my mistakes. I could have chosen joy always, but there were times when I didn't do so. I chose to wallow in self-pity. I chose to focus on the things that made me unhappy, when really my life is filled with infinite blessings. If I had seen that more clearly, I would have spared myself a great deal of sorrow. I could have soared on the wings of eagles."

I tell my kids: "One of the tragedies of being human is that we often appreciate the good things only when, God forbid, we lose them, and that we're rendered indifferent to everything we have— while we have it. Where is the logic in that?

"Similarly, where is the logic in choosing to be unhappy? Why opt for unhappiness when you can be happy? It takes very little effort. You may not feel like smiling, but if you force yourself to smile, the transformation is almost immediate. I know this from personal experience. The greatest antidote to unhappiness is activity. Happiness is about taking control."

As Abraham Lincoln put it, "Most folks are as happy as they make up their minds to be."

Happiness keeps children young. It keeps *adults* young. When you are happy, you overlook slights, you find the good in people, you feel unfettered, you rediscover your innocence—and you want that feeling to last forever. I want my children to love their childhood so it will last, so that the roots will take hold. An unhappy child moves forward too quickly, and abandons his inner child, and runs the risk of becoming like so many broken men and women today—hard-boiled and disconnected.

I often counsel depressed teenagers and find it astonishing that so many of them feel so hopeless. It truly saddens me. An alarming number of these kids are cutters. I ask them, "Why do you cut? Can you explain that to me? Why do you cut your skin and make yourself bleed?"

Some of them are surprisingly deep and self-aware. "I do it in order to feel," one boy told me. "I'm so numb that it's the only way I can feel." Or, from a young woman: "I need some external manifestation of my internal unhappiness. This reflects what I really feel deep inside."

I tell some of these kids, "You can look at this as a chemical imbalance, and see a doctor about it, and he'll undoubtedly medicate you and help you deal with it. But that will begin a cycle of dependency from which you might never break free. Or you can try to regain control of your emotions, on your own, and choose joy. And it *is* a choice. You need to think about the things that are making you unhappy, and about the things that make you happy, and move from one sphere to the next, from the darkness to the light. I have seen people do it. It happens every day."

My son Mendy once came to me and said he wasn't happy because he didn't have a lot of friends. "The kids at school don't like me and never throw me the football during recess," he told me.

I said to him, "Number One, never give someone the key to your self-esteem. Never allow anyone to determine whether you're a happy person or not. The fact that you don't feel you have enough friends is an important subject, and I'm glad we're talking about it, but you can't let other kids determine your self-worth. Don't give someone that power. You know you're a valuable person, so no one can take that away from you. Never put the locus of your self-esteem outside of yourself. It's not in the hands of those other boys, it's in your hands.

"Number Two, there will always be people you don't want to be friends with, and you need to figure out who those people are. Friendship is not the necessity; the *right* friendship is the necessity. If you were living in a place with only wicked people, you would be forced to forgo the whole notion of friendship, because you wouldn't want to spend time around those people. If your friends are cold and distant, try to warm them up. And if that doesn't work, find people who reciprocate your love and joy.

"Finally, here's the thing about unhappiness. The way you feel right now, that those boys reject you and make you unhappy, you can turn that into joy. You can find another neglected kid in school and befriend him. Do something joyous with that unhappiness. You know what it feels like to be left out, so make sure no one else feels the same way. You can go joyously to that other boy and say, 'Hey! Let's be friends. I'm not playing football with anyone else either. Let's you and I play!' You can conquer that negativity. You are the master of it. You can turn it into something joyous."

HAPPINESS IS A CRITICAL COMPONENT OF CHILDHOOD. IT MAKES CHILDHOOD LAST, AND IT KEEPS CHILDREN YOUNG INTO ADULTHOOD AND BEYOND.

I cannot stress this enough: *Happiness is a critical component of childhood.* It makes childhood last, and it keeps children young into adulthood and beyond. The child who is truly a child is blessed, and the parent who helps his child remain a child for as long as possible is himself a blessing.

As a parent, your job is to raise a child that lasts forever, even into that child's old age.

3

KNOWLEDGE AND
INSPIRATION

TO ME, THE TRULY IMPORTANT QUESTION IS
THIS: "ARE YOU INTELLECTUALLY CURIOUS?"

There's a famous expression in the *Zohar*, or the *Book of Illumination*, which is the Bible of the Kabbalah: *The pinnacle of knowledge is to know that you don't know.* In other words, the more you study a subject, the more you see its vastness. The ignorant man thinks he knows everything, but the scholarly man knows how little he knows.

When Socrates was told that he had been singled out by the oracle at Delphi as the smartest man in the world, he chuckled and said, "If that's true, it's because I'm the only man who knows that he doesn't know."

As kids grow up, they tend to act as if they know everything: "Yeah, yeah! You don't have to tell me! I know that already!" They exaggerate facts and invent stories.

Interestingly enough, very young children know that they don't know (just as they know that living in the present is the right way to live). But as they move toward adulthood, they become self-conscious about their lack of knowledge, and their fear of appearing ignorant often makes them stop asking questions.

> ❧
>
> THERE ARE PLENTY OF GOOD SOURCES—MORAL, ETHICAL, RELIGIOUS, SPIRITUAL—BUT NOTHING CAN REPLACE A PARENT.
>
> ❧

To me, this is tragic. A child must never close himself off to advice and guidance. Throughout his life, he will need direction and inspiration. There are plenty of good sources—moral, ethical, religious, spiritual—but nothing can replace a parent.

When one of my children thinks he knows everything about a given topic, I often go out of my way to dig up all sorts of new information, which I then share with him. The object here is not to humiliate the child. On the contrary, I do it for two good reasons: One, to show him that I am interested in his interests. And two, to impress upon him that one never stops learning.

Children do not like to be tested or put on the spot. When a kid comes home with a bad report card, the idea of showing it to his parents is sheer torture. And frankly, I feel for him. I think we put altogether too much stock in academics, and I often wish our schools had a more holistic approach to education. To me, a straight-A student is exactly that: a straight-A student. No more, no less.

I always tell my kids, "I honestly couldn't care less about your grades. It is absolutely meaningless to me." And it's true. I really don't care.

First of all, if we're speaking empirically here, many of our most successful entrepreneurs are college dropouts: Bill Gates, Steve Jobs, and Larry Ellison, to name just three. I'm sure there are a great many more dropouts who are wildly *un*successful, but that's not my point: My point is simply that there is more to life than grades. Every American knows that Abraham Lincoln never went to school, and that George Washington had very little formal education, but they still did pretty well for themselves—right?

I tell my kids, "For me, grades are nothing but a measure of one thing, and a very narrow measure at that. I don't measure success by grades, and you shouldn't either. To me, the more important question is this: *Are you intellectually curious? Do you want to know?*

"All I want to know is that you want to know," I tell them. "Intellectual curiosity is the essence of a good life. Intellectual indolence, on the other hand, can be deadly—both figuratively and literally.

"Intellectual curiosity is one of the great blessings. Boredom, on the other hand, is one of the biggest curses. People who aren't curious, people who don't hunger for life, are dulled by their lack of interest and lack of appetite. They become diminished and intellectually smaller, almost literally shrinking into themselves. Why would anyone choose that dull path when the world has so much to offer?"

People lose interest in people, too, I tell them, and the results are tragic. Curiosity is the soul of every relationship, I explain. The desire to know is the foundation of every interaction we have in life.

"A woman came to see me a few days ago," I told them recently. "She said her husband is no longer interested in her. When he comes home, she begins to tell him about her day, and he turns on the TV. When they sit down to dinner, she tries to make pleasant conversation but again he ignores her and turns his attention to the newspaper.

"Do you know what has happened in this marriage? What has happened is that the man is no longer interested in his wife. As far as he's concerned, there is nothing she can tell him that he hasn't heard already. He has ceased to be curious about her, and his lack of curiosity and interest is killing the marriage."

I tell my kids about Robert Nozik, the celebrated Harvard philosopher. He maintained that most wars throughout history were fought largely over boredom. Yes, *boredom*. It was excess testosterone: men sitting around with nothing to engage their energy or interests. They were bored, so they went out in search of excitement, in search of glory, and ended up slaughtering each other. Life can be boring at times, if you're not careful, but war is *never* boring. War breaks up the routine.

We create wars in our own lives, too, and partly for the same reason: to break up the routine, to shake things up. And this happens in many marriages: People create drama to escape monotony. Their lives are so predictable, so routine, that the drama becomes a source of thrills and excitement, and before long they have killed the marriage. On the other hand, if you're intellectually curious—about life, about people, about each other—this is much less likely to happen.

I say to my kids all the time, "The essence of life is to make ordinary things extraordinary, to make the natural miraculous, and to make the everyday unique."

For me, intellectual curiosity is the essence of a good life, and the essence of good relationships. When you're curious about life, hungry to know more, you will never be challenged by the great bane of existence—boredom. And when you're curious about another person, you will always remain fully engaged with that person. You'll want to know what they've been doing all day, what they're thinking, and what they want to do that weekend. That person will never bore you.

> ❧
> THE ESSENCE OF LIFE IS TO MAKE ORDINARY THINGS EXTRAORDINARY, TO MAKE THE NATURAL MIRACULOUS, AND TO MAKE THE EVERYDAY UNIQUE.
> ❧

Without intellectual curiosity, we are lost.

I said this wasn't a prescriptive book, and it isn't, but we can't very well live without rules. One of the rules in our home is that there's no watching TV during the week. On Saturday, after sundown, when the Sabbath ends, the family sometimes gets together and watches a video or DVD. I let the kids choose, within reason, but I try to discourage them from watching action movies and science fiction or fantasy. The reason for this is simple: *Life itself is interesting.* I don't want them to lose their appreciation for everyday magic. I think the most intelligent films are the ones that are about normal life. If I have to choose between *Terms of Endearment* and *Star Wars*, there's no contest. I can connect with, and respond to, the former because it's about real people, real life, and real situations.

Kids today have lost the capacity to be intrigued by life, in part because they are overstimulated by the make-believe, and their parents seem to be losing it, too. If a kid has an eighty-year-old grandmother, a woman who has lived a full, rich, sometimes tragic life, why isn't he sufficiently interested in listening to her stories? It is a symbol of the magnitude of our failure as parents that the average kid is infinitely more interested in playing with his Xbox than in learning what his grandparents did during the Second World War.

There is a very famous verse in the book of Deuteronomy, which I often discuss with my kids. Moses is speaking to the Jewish people on the last day of his life, lecturing them, getting ready to relinquish his leadership and pass the torch to Joshua. "When I die," he says, as interpreted by the Talmud, "there will be times when God's law, the Torah, will feel empty to you; you will feel that it is boring, not stimulating. Whenever you feel that way, you must remember that the emptiness comes not from the Torah, not from God's law, but from you. The barrenness comes from inside you. You are the ones who are empty. It's *all* interesting. You are the ones who just don't see it."

The message is simple: Life depends on intellectual curiosity. I talk to my kids about this tirelessly. "I have only one major thing going for me," I tell them. "If someone were to say to me, 'Shmuley, what's your greatest virtue?' I would say, 'Intellectual curiosity.' That's what has sustained me. People fascinate me. Why people *do* things fascinates me. History fascinates me. God fascinates me. America fascinates me. Judaism fascinates me. The Christian faith fascinates me. The Islamic faith fascinates me."

At our home, on most evenings at the dinner table I do pop quizzes and my children have grown

> KIDS TODAY HAVE LOST THE CAPACITY TO BE INTRIGUED BY LIFE, IN PART BECAUSE THEY ARE OVERSTIMULATED BY THE MAKE-BELIEVE.

to love it, becoming trivia buffs in the process. History, geography, politics—maybe something I read in the paper that morning. And I make it fun because it's my job to awaken their interest. These nonstop quizzes, which continue on hikes or on long drives, have led to an interesting result: My kids may not have the highest grades in their class, but they are universally acknowledged to have the largest amount of information. And this is a direct result of having internalized the desire to know.

If one night at dinner I see they're not in the mood for a quiz, I'll bring something else to the table, something I can share with the entire family. It could be a forthcoming segment from my television show that I hope will spark debate: "What is motivating this husband to be so cruel to his wife?" "Why does this eighteen-year-old girl never speak to her mother about her boyfriend?" "Why is this boy so sullen?"

But you don't need your own television show to stimulate your children. Life itself is exciting. A businessman might come home and tell his kids about a real-estate deal that went sour. He can describe the principal players, and he can describe the terms of the deal, and he can tell them where it fell apart. He makes a simple business transaction come alive for them, awakening their curiosity.

The ordinary becomes extraordinary. *These are the people involved in the deal. This is how it fell apart. What do you think happened? What was the straw that broke the camel's back?*

A mother can talk about a friend with whom she had a falling out. She can take the kids back to the day she first met this friend, to the reasons they became friends, and, finally, she can describe the events that caused the friendship to crumble. That, to me, is better than any episode on television, and much more exciting: after all, one of the principal players is in the room!

Nowadays, it seems as if families have stopped talking to each other, and when they do talk, the conversations usually remain on the surface of life. But if you foster an appetite for depth early in a child's life, it will have a tremendous effect on his future. Your son will look for a deeper kind of woman. Your daughter will find a man with the types of subtle qualities that often go unappreciated. (Nice guys *do* get overlooked from time to time!) A child who has the ability to look deeper, who is attuned to the world around him, has a far greater chance of becoming a success than a child with an indolent mind.

When I talk to my children about the characters I meet as I go about my day, or about the people who appear on my television show, my goal is to *get them interested.* I want them to become students of human nature. What motivates people? What drives their actions? What destroys their lives and leads them to make the wrong decisions?

I don't believe in sheltering my kids, and I'm not sure I could shelter them even if I wanted to. They hear about marital breakups, they're familiar with tragedy, and they know that the world has been polluted by hatred and war. Instead of denying reality, I try to give them the tools to handle, and hopefully, change it. Kids are genuinely curious, and it is part of your job as a parent to foster that curiosity, and to make them even more curious.

"Why are there evil people in the world, Daddy?"

You could sidestep this question; it's a tough one. "Well, there just are, son. But you don't have to worry about it—you live in New Jersey. Now finish your vegetables." But why not capitalize on your child's interest and use to the opportunity to broaden his mind?

"Well, baby girl, there was a very famous German philosopher named Georg Hegel, and he often talked about something he described as the *thymotic urge.* That sounds complicated, but it's not. Hegel believed that the greatest human desire was to be recognized, that we all want to be respected by our peers—that we hunger to have our accomplishments and our uniqueness appreciated by equals.

"Hegel pointed out that animals will risk their lives for food, but humans will risk their lives for recognition. We see this in professional athletes, many of whom gladly endanger life and limb for fame and fortune. And we see it in titans of business, who can be relentless in their pursuit of wealth and fame: *Look at me! Notice me!* Then there are people who want recognition so badly that they seek it out at any cost. A murderer often hungers to get caught because if no one knows what he did he will remain unrecognized."

"Don't *you* want recognition?"

"As a matter of fact, *I* do. As much as the next man. Maybe more so. Your father has his own insecurities, and he often looks to outsiders for approval. To be completely honest, I have sought recognition my whole life. I've wanted people to know me and to appreciate my unique gifts, and I've wanted to inspire them. But I also want to be recognized for being authentic, for trying to inspire goodness in others, and that is more important to me than my desire for recognition. I am genuinely driven to do good because I believe in doing good, in doing right—even when no one is looking, and maybe *especially* when no one is looking."

Of course, I don't always succeed. One of the things I have struggled with my whole life is my fear of failure and mediocrity. And it still colors much of what I do. But I don't believe in hiding my shortcomings from my children. I believe that part of the reason they respect me is that they can see me struggling to become a better man, a better husband, and a better father.

I tell my kids, "I have taken thousands of hours from my time with you to write books, produce shows, deliver lectures, and meet with influential people. Part of this is because it's how I make my living, but part of it is my continuing thirst for recognition, albeit for good things. I still want to be special, but I want to be special to you kids most of all. And that's why I will keep working on myself to always make sure that you guys come first in my life, because you are absolutely first in my heart."

Certainly, we all want to distinguish ourselves, even if it's only to compensate for our insecurities. But we need to distinguish ourselves as parents first. If you focus exclusively on your professional life, you might be a hero at the office, but you'll be a zero at home. That eight-year-old you're neglecting today could very well demand a great deal of attention from you in his teens (probably the wrong kind of attention!). And think about it: Have you really been a success in life if the people who mean the most to you think the least of you?

Parents often come to me and say, "You make it sound so easy, but I'm not a rabbi or a talk-show host or a philosopher. I don't know how to talk to my kids! I don't know how to get them excited about learning!"

"Everything is learning," I tell them. "On the way to the grocery store today, you heard an interesting debate on the radio. While you were in the grocery store, a belligerent man got into an argument with a meek woman at the express check-out lane because she had more than twelve items. And on your way home, you saw a dog-catcher chasing a homeless dog down the street. There are stories behind all of these stories. Who was that belligerent man? What kind of person would embarrass a stranger in a grocery store? And who was he really angry at? It couldn't have been that meek woman.

"And what about the dog-catcher? What a strange way to make a living, chasing animals, day in, day out. And how does he feel about animals? Does he like them? Does he treat them well? Does

> ❧
>
> EVERYTHING THAT HAPPENS IN YOUR LIFE PROVIDES AN OPPORTUNITY FOR CONVERSATION WITH YOUR CHILDREN. YOU JUST HAVE TO TRAIN YOURSELF TO SEE IT.
>
> ❧

he have pets of his own? And why do people have pets, anyway? Is it because we're lonely? And what about all those people who seem closer to their pets than to people?"

Everything that happens in your life provides an opportunity for conversation with your children. You just have to train yourself to see it. It is *all* interesting. It is up to you to make it so. You can do it with an extra twenty minutes at the dinner table. And here's the thing: *It doesn't have to be preachy.* If one of my kids does something wrong, I might take him behind closed doors and give him a good talking to, but more often than not I use everyday occurrences to start conversations with him. Something memorable or inspiring happens in the course of the day, and it becomes fodder for communication. It's about reacting to life, and it's about showing our kids that—if one looks—opportunities for reflection and inspiration are everywhere. The trick is not to let these moments pass us by.

And trust me, I know what it's like—I have eight kids, thank God. Most families tend to rush through dinner, especially the kids. They can't wait to get back to their computers and cell phones and iPods. *But they'll stick around if the conversation is interesting.* And the biggest determinant is *you.* If you see yourself and your life as a crashing bore, your kids will see the same thing. But if you see your life as an endless succession of miraculous and fascinating events, your kids will be transformed by it.

It's not limited to the dinner table, either. I may not know much about opera or ballet, but I love to read, and I think reading is a critical component of an inspired life, so once or twice a month I take all the kids to the local bookstore. I try to direct them to the types of books I like—historical biographies, for example—but if they prefer Harry Potter I'm not going to complain. I will try and steer them toward books that are inspired by real people and events, but as long as they're reading I'm a happy man.

Of course, if I see an opportunity to get them to read something I really want them to read, I try to take it. Last year, for example, I took the family to visit Graceland, and I picked up a wonderful book about Elvis, *Last Train to Memphis*. It had all the elements of a Greek tragedy, and I found it so gripping that I found myself reading passages aloud to the family. The kids ended up arguing about who had dibs on the book when I was done, and eventually three of them read it. It taught them an incredible lesson: *Success can be just as corrosive as failure*.

In the days ahead, our dinner table discussions became very lively.

"Elvis had tremendous success, but it still wasn't enough," I observed at one point. "I find that fascinating because to me that is one of life's great mysteries: When is enough enough? Why are we insatiable? Are we ever truly satisfied?"

When you can discuss these types of things with your children, you are doing your job as a parent. You're discussing humanity, discussing human strengths and weakness, interpreting motivation—and it's all interesting. Such conversations make the world come alive for a child, and they awaken his intellectual curiosity—and that's the objective.

My kids had been to Graceland, so the subject resonated for them. If I had told them to read an academic book about the fall of the Roman Empire and have a report on my desk by Sunday night, I don't think I would have seen much enthusiasm. But by seeking out a subject that engaged their interest, I had them hooked.

And there is no shortage of material. The world *is* interesting. I often turn to the newspaper for inspiration. As the host of a talk-show, I live and die by current events, so I start my day by reading two newspapers, clipping articles, then calling my producer to figure out which ones we're going to concentrate on that day. When I get home in the evening, and the family is gathered around the dinner table, I will often mention one or two of these stories, hoping to engage the kids. In seeking out their opinions, I am not only trying to stimulate their developing intellects, but I'm letting them know that I'm interested in what they have to say.

I do the same thing when we go on vacation. Last summer, we piled into the family RV and spent six weeks on the road. We went to the Little Rock Central High School, and my children learned how the forcible desegregation of that school in 1957 impacted the entire country. I took them to see the Lorraine Motel, in Memphis, where Martin Luther King was shot in April 1968. Standing together at the site, we read the hauntingly appropriate Biblical words, originally written of Joseph, on the marble slab erected there in Martin Luther King's memory: "And they said to each other, Behold, the dreamer cometh. Come let us slay him . . . and we shall see what will become of his dreams."

We went to the Mississippi coast to visit Beauvoir, the home of Jefferson Davis, the only president of the Confederacy, and we talked about the turbulent times that shaped this country in one of its darkest hours. We even went to New Orleans, just months before Hurricane Katrina devastated the city, and visited the Chalmette Battlefield, where Andrew Jackson crushed the British in January of 1815.

Do my kids always find all of this as fascinating as I do? Definitely not. But my efforts have turned them into intellectually curious kids. When *Time* and *Newsweek* arrive at the house, for example, they scramble to read them first. That pleases me greatly, especially since my son, Mendy, at age twelve, is often more familiar with current events than I am. In a day and age when most kids can't get excited about anything beyond the hot new video game, or what everyone is doing on Saturday night, my children are intrigued by, and have an appetite for, the world around them.

A parent's job is to expand a child's horizons. Hanging out in front of the TV or playing video games with them is better than nothing, but it's hardly a philosophy of parenting. Our job is to inspire our kids to maximize their fullest potential. To dig deeper. If your son is interested in baseball, talk to him about the recent steroid scandal. ("Why would a man risk all by taking steroids? What price are we prepared to pay for success? What constitutes a true hero?") I do my humble best to make them look deeper, to peer under the hood, as it were.

The conversations that stimulate your children will stay with them. When I talked to my children about steroids, they referred back to our conversation about the thymotic urge. "People need to be noticed! They'll do anything to get noticed! And when you can hit the ball out of the park like that, you'll get noticed."

"But when is it enough?" I ask my kids, "Do you know what the greatest destroyer of mankind is? It's his insatiability. Nothing is ever enough. You're not pretty enough. You're not making enough money. Your house is too small. Your neighbor has a faster Porsche. *Why is it never enough?*" In this manner, we take a simple conversation about baseball and transform it into a great deal more.

A few nights later, we were back on the subject of man's insatiability, and I found myself again talking to my children about Adam and Eve: "As I interpret it, they are adults who are really children, so they're perfect, and their perfection lies in the perfect synthesis of their adult and childlike virtues. As adults, they are responsible and intelligent and developed, but they've lost none of their childhood innocence. So they run around naked and unashamed and *content*. And that's the reason they're in Paradise—because they are *content*. Contentment is a pretty good definition of Paradise, don't you think? If we read a story to your little brother, that's enough. If we play with him, that's enough. That's because he hasn't yet been bitten by the serpent, which is what ruined Paradise for Adam and Eve. And what is the serpent? The classical, Jewish interpretation is that the serpent is a metaphor for *insatiability*. The snake slithers along the ground eating dust, which is plentiful but never satisfying, and so the serpent remains hungry always. Now he spreads his insatiability by biting Eve and putting that same poison into her, and she in turn passes it on to Adam. They become cold, just as a person who is bitten by a real snake becomes cold when the poison begins to take effect. And the coldness robs them of their passion. Nothing excites them anymore. Not even each other. Not the bounty that surrounds them. Only the forbidden fruit captures their interest, and so they become fixated on what they can't have. And that is how it begins. Adam and Eve become adults who are consumed by a deprivation mentality. This is what drives them out of the Garden. They will never be satisfied. Paradise is lost to them.

"And that is the lesson here: *Learn to be satisfied.*"

I have many shortcomings as a parent, but one of my strengths is that I holistically pursue the intellectual development of my children, and one of the ways I do this is by including them in absolutely everything and anything I find interesting. And it goes well beyond books and the newspaper stories. Embrace knowledge and you embrace life.

Oh, I know: Parents today complain that their kids don't want to talk to them, but who's running the show? There are two approaches to parenting. The short, long way would be: "What did you do at school today?" And the answer will be: "Nothing. It was just a regular day." The long, short way would be to do your homework as a parent and bring something of interest to the table. "I was driving home today and I heard a story about the Flying Wallendas, one of the most famous high-wire acts of all time. Did you know that they always worked *without* a safety net?"

"Wow! Were any of them ever hurt?"

"Hurt?! Are you kidding? Several of them were *killed*."

"No!"

"I wonder why they risked their lives for their art? Who would do a thing like that? What kind of risks do *we* take in our daily lives? When is a risk worth taking, and when is it not worth taking, and how do we know the difference?"

The most important weekly tradition in our orthodox Jewish household—and a great opportunity for family conversation—is the Shabbat dinner, which is celebrated every Friday night. It is observed just before sundown, and it begins a day of rest, or of "ceasing" from work. We always have many guests, and in most households I notice that kids run away from the table, because they don't enjoy adult company and conversation, and aren't expected to enjoy it. But my kids don't do that. They seldom ask to leave the table because adult subjects are not foreign to them, and because human beings interest them. "Every person has a story, and every story is interesting," I always tell them. "Life is fascinating. If you listen intently, everyone has something to say, and you can learn from everyone you meet."

When you no longer find other people interesting, your life becomes diminished, and you are touched by less. If you let this happen to your children, they will begin to live their lives vicariously, through the fantasy mediums of movies, television, and video games, and they will lose their connection to other people.

"Only connect," the British writer E.M. Forster wrote in *Howard's End*.

Only connect! That was the whole of her sermon.
Only connect the prose and the passion, and both
will be exalted,
And human love will be seen at its height.
Live in fragments no longer.
Only connect . . .

But maybe we should *dis*connect—from our computers, from our cell phones, from our iPods, from our plasma televisions and our BlackBerrys and our Palm Pilots—so that we can reconnect with humanity.

I am suddenly reminded of something Karl Wallenda once said of his life as a trapeze artist: "Being on the wire is living. Everything else is waiting." Well, that's a bit cynical for me. I'd like to think that *living* is being on the wire. If you're interested in the world around you, there is no waiting.

4

BESTOWING DIGNITY

EVERY HUMAN BEING HAS VALUE,
AND EVERY HUMAN ENCOUNTER IS A
FRESH CHANCE TO LET HIM KNOW IT.

The most essential human necessity is not food, water, clothing, or shelter, but dignity. People need dignity to survive. When you rob a person of his dignity, you are robbing him of his will to live.

Whenever my children are confused about their place in the world, or their mission in life, I am always very clear on this point. I tell them, "Some people will say your mission is to practice kindness. Some will say it is to respect life. Some believe it is to love and be loved. But your foremost mission in life is to confer dignity on all of God's creatures." This is the message I drill into my children's heads, and it is the subject of recurring conversations in our home. "You are bestowers of dignity. That is your foremost role."

I elaborate on the theme: "God gave you an infinite supply of dignity to bestow on other human beings. You are a dignity-giver. Within your person you possess one of the most incredible abilities of all—the power to make people feel special, that they truly matter—and it is your job to do so. Over the course of your life, you must try to bestow dignity on as many people as you can."

There is no greater gift than bestowing dignity, no greater contentment than to know that you have done so, no greater achievement than to establish the nobility of every person you meet.

> ❧
> YOUR FOREMOST MISSION
> IN LIFE IS TO CONFER
> DIGNITY ON ALL OF GOD'S
> CREATURES.
> ❧

To be sure, most children only have a vague understanding of the meaning of dignity. It is a concept they must acquire. They themselves often behave in a highly undignified manner. They humiliate each other, fight, argue, scream, and much worse, so they need to be made aware of how essential dignity is, both for themselves and for others. You can literally change the life of a person by bestowing dignity, and you can change your own life by behaving with dignity. Because I sincerely believe this, I often talk to my children about the meaning of dignity and about the connection between dignity and morality.

I have a dear friend in Los Angeles, Dennis Prager, the wise talk-show host and author, and he always says, "The way to gauge someone's morality is to see how they treat the people they don't need." I am wholly in agreement with that statement, and I have tried to impress that on my children.

When I was the rabbi at Oxford University in England, for example, we hired *au pairs* from time to time to help us with our growing family. We needed the help, and, fortunately, we were able to afford it, and the women who came in and out of our lives were usually from the neighborhood or from other wealthy, western European countries. Most of them were similar to us in education, background, and skin color, and they fit seamlessly into the family.

> THE WAY TO GAUGE SOMEONE'S MORALITY IS TO SEE HOW THEY TREAT THE PEOPLE THEY DON'T NEED.

When we returned to the United States in 1999, however, a lot changed. The women in our employ usually spoke Spanish, and they were culturally and physically removed from our kids. I soon discovered that most Americans simply assume that the "help" belongs to another class, and to a lower class at that. Many of these women had children of their own, and in order to make a living they had to become separated from their families, sometimes for years at a time, while they sent money home.

"I want all of you to think about who these women are," I told my children one night at dinner. "They are mothers themselves, and they have to be far away from their children in order to support them. Can you imagine how painful that is for a mother? They're here taking care of you kids while someone else is taking care of theirs. I want you to remember that at all times. Life isn't always fair, and these women aren't as fortunate as we are, but you must never think they have less value than you do. You must always treat them as your equals. They are equally God's children."

I told my children about Immanuel Kant, and how he struggled his whole life to define the concept of morality. In his view, a person was guilty of immorality if he treated a fellow human being as a means to an end. You could not set one standard for yourself and another for the rest of humanity, he said. The moral person saw his fellow human beings as equals, and he treated them accordingly.

I endeavor to live by this philosophy, and I want my children to live by it as well. I expect my children to treat all their fellow human beings with an equal measure of respect. "Everyone deserves dignity by their very birthright," I always remind them. "The woman who works in our home has as much value as a visiting politician, and the politician has no more value than a waiter, a cab driver, or the man who delivers our mail. No one—not a single person on the planet—must ever be made to feel inferior."

Not long ago, my wife Debbie and I went away for a few days. When we returned, the young woman who worked for us at the time came to me, with tears in her eyes, and said that one of the children had been verbally abusive to her during our absence. I brought my kids into the dining room and sat them down. I was upset and disappointed. "I never would have believed that you would be the kind of children who could make this young woman feel as if she is beneath you," I said. "This woman does a job, just like your father does a job. I struggle to write for a living. She helps with our household for a living. No one is better than anyone else. Every job honestly performed is noble and majestic. How is it possible that your behavior has brought this young woman to tears? If you saw someone else doing that, what would you conclude?"

My kids are not spoiled—we are not a wealthy family—but these things can happen in any family, and it is the responsibility of the parent to see that they don't.

Let me give you another example from my own family. Late in 2004, I was on my way to Manhattan for the launch of my book, *Face Your Fear*, and my eldest daughter, Mushki, came with me. There was a lot of traffic, and the taxi driver said he knew a shortcut. Well, the shortcut ended up being three times as long. I was very angry and deeply upset, but I knew he had been trying to do me a favor, so I controlled my response. He kept apologizing, but I told him not to worry, to do the best he could to get us there in good time. "These things happen," I said, and I engaged him in conversation.

It turned out that the driver and his wife had just had a child, and I asked about the child, and since we were sitting in traffic, not moving, he showed me pictures of the newborn. I looked at the pictures and said all the right things, smiling at the man, but on the inside I was burning up at him for making me late to my own book launch.

When we finally arrived, I paid the driver, thanked him a bit too profusely, then hurried inside with Mushki. I gave my speech, signed copies of my book, talked to friends and well-wishers, and two hours later my daughter and I were in another cab, on our way home.

I soon discovered that Mushki had been thinking about that first cab ride the entire evening, and as soon as we were alone, in the back of this second cab, she brought it up. She told me that she had been very upset with the driver, and that she hadn't understood why I had said nothing. I turned in my seat and looked at her. "Do you know why I behaved the way I behaved?" I asked. "Believe me, I wanted to yell my head off at him, but I have always felt torn between two things: my morality and my ambition. Tonight was a big night for me—*An author! Signing copies of his new book!*—but I have never wanted my desire for personal success to color the way I treat other people. I don't want to become one of those despicable men who will callously step on others to get ahead. If I succeed by taking that route, I will be a rank failure.

"The cab driver had been trying to help us by taking a shortcut, and it was a mistake, and I was very angry—and that's why I had to work especially hard at being nice to him. *Because I am here to give people dignity, not rob them of it.* I may have felt like raising my voice to him—'Listen to me, you S.O.B., I need to get to my book launch! You got us lost, now find your way out of this mess!'—but I couldn't do it. Had I done so, I would have been putting my desire for success before my morality, and I would have felt like a failure as a human being. I would have become one of those disgusting people who treat others like garbage. So I did the opposite of what I felt: I made conversation with him, and I looked at pictures of his newborn, and I tried to connect with him. And I made a special effort because you were in the car with me."

"I don't understand," Mushki said.

"I wanted to show you by example. The driver got us lost, yes, but he's still a person, and the only thing that really matters—*the only thing*—is to treat others with dignity, even if, and perhaps *especially* if, they get in the way of your ambition.

"In life, you must always work at connecting with other people. Whenever I climb into a taxi, I don't just climb into a taxi. I try to say hello to the driver and acknowledge him. I want him to know that he's not simply the guy who has to get me from Point A to Point B, but a human brother. It is immoral to treat others as a means to an end."

I want to foster in my children the idea that everyone is special, so that they'll carry that with them into the world. When we have guests to our home, for example, my children are expected to greet people as they come in the door, and to make them feel truly welcome. A simple hello is not enough. I want my children to look each guest in the eye, to really *see* him, and to recognize something that is uniquely his.

"Dignity is like an invisible cloak, and it protects us," I tell my children. "But when we are shamed, the cloak disappears, and we feel naked without it. So you must actively protect the dignity of every person with whom you come into contact. By acknowledging another person, by making them know they matter, you are conferring value. To do otherwise is to rob them of dignity and, consequently, of self-respect. Do that often enough and you rob a person of their will to live.

"Words are powerful. God created the world through words: 'Let there be light. Let there be a firmament.' Well, words can 'create' people, too. When you smile at someone, or tell them how good they look, or ask about their day, you are conferring dignity. You bring them to life. Whenever you make someone feel they matter, you lend them dignity. When you listen to someone, you give them the gift of dignity. We are defined by our ability to bestow dignity. Bestowing dignity is part of your reason for being."

I remember going to lunch with a businessman who wanted to collaborate on a project, and the moment the waitress appeared I questioned whether this project would be moving forward. I was really turned off by the imperious, patronizing manner with which he spoke to the waitress, and I decided I didn't really want to be in business with a jerk. In the course of lunch, when we spoke, I could see he wasn't really listening to me. He was not interested in anything I had to say, and he kept interrupting to talk about himself. That's not *listening*. When you truly listen to someone, you must completely abandon your agenda for that period of time—three minutes, ten minutes, an hour—and focus only on them. Listening is one way of conferring true dignity, and good listeners create authentic relationships.

To illustrate the point, I told my kids a story about Albert Reichman, the billionaire Canadian real-estate magnate—a story that my own father had told me almost twenty years earlier. "As an Orthodox Jew, Reichman tended to dress and look like a rabbi. One day, he arrived at the office of an important Manhattan executive, and the assistant mistook him for a rabbi. Even though he professed to have an appointment, he didn't immediately volunteer his name, and the assistant told her boss that a rabbi was outside, probably eager to collect funds for one cause or another. Her boss said, 'Get rid of him. He's here to *schnorr* money. They all claim to have an appointment.' When the secretary asked him to leave, Reichman was perplexed. 'But I don't understand,' he said. 'Please tell him that Albert Reichman is waiting for him.' Flabbergasted at her error, the secretary apologized profusely and ushered Reichman into the office, where her mortified boss also apologized for the mistake. Reichman accepted the apology, but said that the deal was off. As he was turning to leave, the executive asked why he was being so harsh. 'I've already apologized for my mistake,' he whined.

" 'You don't understand,' Reichman said. 'I'm not calling off the deal because you insulted me. I'm calling off the deal because you insulted the average, ordinary man who comes to your office to see you, and for whom you have no time. You insulted the poor guy on the street who is forced to rely on others to survive. You should treat all men with respect, be they paupers or billionaires.'

"You see?" I told my children. "Albert Reichman really understood the meaning of dignity."

Unfortunately, all of us tend to confer dignity based on some imaginary measure of value. My kids know, for example, that from time to time I do business with influential people. I'm a radio host, and some of my guests are fairly well known; I'm an author, and I sometimes meet with decision makers in publishing; and as the host of a television show I find at times myself conferring with powerful people in the media. But in my own home, I go out of my way to invite the people with whom I feel most comfortable, not those who are deemed influential, but those who are most like me: simple, ordinary people. In my home, status is utterly meaningless. "Every person has infinite value," I tell my children. "By seeking this value out, you are bestowing dignity."

Let me give you an example of what happens when you *fail* to do this. Not long ago, a woman came to one of our Shabbat dinners as the guest of a friend. She was a stranger to us, and everyone treated her with respect, but none of us actively sought to engage her, and I became aware of this late in the evening, as things were winding down. At that point, I turned to her and asked if she had any children, and she took a moment and said, "I had a young daughter who was killed in a car accident. My life has never been the same since, and I have lost my faith in God."

Obviously, the terrible tragedy caught everyone's attention, and we got into a very interesting conversation. She had suffered tragically, turned to God for an explanation, and—when no explanation was forthcoming—she had abandoned Him. Everyone was mesmerized by this woman's story, and my kids hung onto every word.

> THE PEOPLE FROM WHOM YOU EXPECT THE LEAST ARE OFTEN THE ONES WITH THE MOST TO OFFER.

Later, after all the guests had gone home, I turned to them and said, "Did you see what happened this evening? There was a woman at our table, a quiet woman, and nobody spoke to her because they thought she had nothing to say. And really, she was the most interesting person there. She had survived tragedy, and her heart had been broken, and she badly wanted to share her experience with anyone who would listen, to find comfort in our interest. If we hadn't engaged this quiet stranger at our table, we would have been the poorer for it. The lesson to be learned is this: The people from whom you expect the least are often the ones with the most to offer."

One finds opportunities to bestow dignity every day, if only one looks for them. Last summer, for example, about six weeks before Hurricane Katrina hit, the family was on vacation in New Orleans. We were walking though Lafayette Square one night, around ten o'clock, and the only people on the streets at that late hour were palm readers, Tarot card readers, and the homeless. As we were making our way along, a black man approached me, and I noticed he had a brown paper bag in his left hand. I could see a bottle peering out from within the folds.

"Hey, man!" he said. "Got some change?" I stopped walking, reached into my pocket for a dollar, and gave it to him. As I put it into his hand, I said, "Listen, please use it for something good." And he said, "Oh, I will! I will!" And I said, "No, seriously—you're way too smart to blow it on booze, you're way too smart to throw your life away. Try to get back on your feet. You know this isn't who you want to be. I can see that you have a gentle heart." And he said, "Thank you, man! Thank you! God bless you!" And I said, "God bless you, too." Then I rejoined my family and we went on our way.

As soon as we were out of earshot, my daughter said to me, "Why did you give him a dollar when you know he's going to spend it on liquor? You are only corrupting him. You know your words aren't going to help him at all."

And I replied, "I didn't give him a dollar to buy him food or to buy him booze or anything like that. I gave him a dollar because when a man is reduced to asking, he has lost his dignity. None of us, God forbid, should be reduced to asking. There's a Jewish prayer, 'Please help us that we never have to ask anyone for our daily bread.' I gave that man a dollar to show him that I wouldn't walk by him as if he didn't exist, which would have robbed him of his last shred of dignity. I wanted him to know that he wasn't invisible, and I wanted to acknowledge him as a fellow human being. By giving him a dollar, I bought myself the chance *to confer dignity on him*. And when people feel dignified, they sometimes shape up their lives—they feel as if they have betrayed their own dignity."

"He's probably buying a drink right now," my daughter said.

"It's possible," I said. "And I can't control that. But I did the best I could. I asked him from the bottom of my heart not to waste the money on drink; to stop squandering his life. In taking the time to tell him he had value as a man, I was trying to inspire him to change. I spent less than a minute talking to that man, but who knows? That brief talk might be the catalyst that prompts him to try to get back on his feet."

At the time, I didn't know whether my words had had any impact on my kids, but a few days later we were in Vicksburg, Mississippi, and I had to stop to do my radio show. So I parked the RV, gave each of the children ten dollars in spending money, and sent them on their way together.

When my daughters returned later in the afternoon, Chana told me that she and Mushki had run into a homeless man on the street, and that Mushki had given him her entire ten dollars. "She gave him the exact same lecture you gave that other man," she said. "She asked him not to spend the money on alcohol, and she urged him to try to get off the streets."

Two days later, we were in Little Rock, Arkansas, and by this time it seemed as if my kids were actively looking for homeless people to give money to. Now I must say, I am not actively trying to raise a family of Mother Teresa wannabees, but I felt pretty darn good about this development. Our many conversations about dignity, coupled with seeing the philosophy being put into practice, had had a powerful effect on them. It forever changed the way they would look at homeless people. And it wasn't even about the *outcome*. We will never know whether we changed the lives of any of those people, but we will always know we tried.

Man cannot live without dignity, nor should he live without making every effort to confer it on others.

I tell my children: "Every human being has value, and every human encounter is a fresh chance to let him know it."

5

HONORING THE FEMININE

WOMEN NURTURE AND ENHANCE EVERYTHING
THEY COME INTO CONTACT WITH,
MEN MOST OF ALL.

As the father of five daughters, I often worry about the direction in which the world is moving. For thousands of years, history was very masculine and aggressive. We had the Greek Empire, the Roman Empire, Attila the Hun, Genghis Khan—a world that was all about brute strength. Men lived by the sword and became known for their violent exploits. Little by little, however, as civilization progressed, allowing spirituality to spread, a more feminine world began to emerge. Suddenly people began to question the old notions. Maybe might didn't make right after all, they said. Maybe we could accomplish more through peacefulness and tenderness and nurturing and relationship-building—all of those wonderful "feminine qualities."

For hundreds of years, civilization continued along that path, the right path, but it seems to be regressing of late—going back to raw masculinity and savagery. This must not happen, and that is why this conversation is one of the essential conversations in the book. Children need to understand what the feminine represents on a much larger scale, in its historical context even. We can't expect them to fully understand it today, now, as children, but we can certainly lay the foundations for it, so that they'll understand it when the time is right.

Let's begin with a brief conversation about the dual nature of God, one that I have often discussed with my older kids. Two of the world's great philosophers, René Descartes and Benedict de Spinoza, had very different opinions regarding God's true nature. Descartes said God created the world and left humanity to its own devices, that He was aloof, detached, and unmovable. Spinoza said God had never abandoned us: that He was everywhere we looked—that He was part of nature itself.

The Kabbalah posits that both philosophers were right. There are in fact two sides to God, it suggests, one masculine, one feminine. The masculine God is the God of history, revealing Himself as strong and determined, a miracle-worker, rewarding the just and punishing the wicked. This God is represented by a straight line. The feminine God is the God of creation, an all-encompassing celestial presence, nursing the universe in Her womb, nurturing, soft-edged, and gentle. This God is represented by a circle.

These two aspects of God—the linear and the circular—are also said to represent the spiritual origins of men and women. Men are a line: their approach to life is very direct and goal-oriented. Women are a circle: less direct, gentler, more open to the world around them, inclined toward circles of family and relationships. Our gender, then, very much determines our approach to life, and this is why we complement each other so perfectly.

The linear approach is too rigid, however, so when a woman comes into man's life she makes him more flexible. "Be a line!" she says. "That's good. I wanted a man. I didn't marry a woman. But be a little bit of a curve, too. Don't be so rigid and stubborn. You don't always have to have your way.

And don't be afraid of commitment. Attach your-self to this circle—I will not confine you."

A woman elevates and redeems a man. She makes him enjoy life, slow down, delight in his children, and seek less goal-oriented pursuits. Women nurture and enhance everything they come into contact with, men most of all. And, in fact, to be completely blunt about it, a man without a woman can sometimes be insufferable. That is why the book of Proverbs says, "A man who has found a woman has found goodness."

This Kabbalistic approach further argues that life is all about balance: the male God of the line and the female God of the circle, the active and the passive—two halves, operating in unison. To ig-nore this is to live a life without balance, and we all know what happens when we lose our balance.

If someone were to ask me to sum up the Jew-ish religion in a single sentence, I would say, "Ju-daism is the cultivation of the feminine." The Jewish people are really the battered wives of the nations of the world. We have always tried to de-velop and cultivate our feminine side. Moses, the greatest prophet in the Bible, refers to himself as a *nursemaid*. King David was a warrior, but his real passion was for the harp and lyre. In fact, if you travel throughout ancient Israel, you won't find a single triumphal arch glorifying a military victory. When the Jews fought, they fought out of necessity, not in the pursuit of glory. Even then, the Jews had a decidedly feminine worldview, and were convinced that one day men would *beat their swords into ploughshares.* Think about that for a moment. It means, quite literally, that lines will be turned into circles; that men will become more feminine; that human rigidity will give way to a new softness; that the nurturer in us will replace the restive warrior.

The prophet Isaiah also spoke of a time when the wolf would lie down with the lamb, and of a time when a child would lead a lion. He believed that the predatory streak in humans and animals would be purged, that human beings would one day learn to get along, and that harmony would prevail. Our whole culture would become more *circular,* he suggested, and the competitively linear quality that so much defines our society—with some people at the top of the totem pole and others at the bottom—would gradually disappear.

I believe this, too, and I believe women will take us there. I speak to my children about this all the time. A woman's gift to the world is her femininity. She takes a cold, desolate planet, warms it with her femininity, and brings forth life. A man's gift to the world is to honor the feminine, and an added obligation is to nurture the feminine in his own heart.

I tell my children, "The world has enough harsh men, and altogether too many masculinized women. This is because the world can be a hard place, and at early age we begin to steel ourselves against the things that hurt us. Divorce, emotional violence, the unkindness of a person we trusted. But if we are afraid to be soft, if we don't honor the feminine within, how will we make the world a kinder, gentler place?

"I want you to grow up to be nurturers, to have soft hearts and kind hands. I want you to be part of the light and gentleness, not the coldness, not the dark."

A few weeks ago, as part of my television show, I visited a family in Connecticut. This was a second marriage for both the father and mother, and each had brought children into the new home. When we met with them, two years into the new marriage, the family was comprised of four girls, ages twenty, eighteen, fourteen, and twelve; an eight-year-old boy; and a new addition, an infant daughter, the result of the new union.

The eight-year-old boy struck me as a broken child. He never smiled. He never showed much joy. He was withdrawn and subdued. Nobody played with him. He seemed abandoned in his own home. One day I asked him, "Do me a favor. Write one page for me about your family."

He wrote the following: "This is my family. I miss my daddy. I only see him every few months. I like my stepfather, but he has no time for me. He plays with my two-year-old sister. Then there's my four sisters. I love them but every time I walk into their room they tell me to get out. If I touch any of their things, they tell me to stop. I try to play with them, but they won't play with me."

I sat down with the four girls and read them the letter, and when I was done I said, "Your brother is so lonely, and you girls are not doing anything about it. There was a time when an older sister was expected to help take care of the family. Girls added gentility and warmth and softness to the home. Why are you girls so harsh? I know you've been through a divorce, but why have you allowed it to harden you? Why are you afraid to be gentle to your own brother, who badly needs you? If you were boys, beating each other to a pulp and giving each other wedgies, I wouldn't condone it, but I'd understand it a bit better. But you're young women! You can't afford to lose the softness."

When I told my kids this story, I summed it up as follows: "These girls had been so hurt by life that they turned their backs on the feminine almost completely."

Later, I sat the boy down in front of his sisters, and I asked him, "Do you want your sisters to love you more?" He nodded. I said, "Why haven't you told them?" He shook his head and shrugged. I asked him, "Is it because it would make you feel weak?" He nodded again, looking shamed and beaten, and I found myself practically begging the girls to reach out to their little brother. How would they ever turn into gentle, loving, *feminine* women if they weren't made aware of how hardened they'd become? They had a deeply skewed sense of femininity, down to the way they dressed: tight, low-cut pants, revealing tops, and gobs of make-up.

Interestingly enough, I was not impervious to some of these very elements in my own home. I remember returning to the house one Friday afternoon, late, to find my eldest daughter Mushki helping her mother set the table for Shabbat dinner. Although only sixteen, Mushki is a very feminine young lady because that's the way we raised her, but on this particular evening I was surprised to see that she was wearing a little too much make-up. I didn't like the way it looked, so I took her aside and sat her down. "Let me explain something to you," I said. "There's selling and there's overselling. If I go to a publisher and say, 'I have the greatest book ever, and it's going to sell ten million copies, and if you publish it I'll have your baby and take your last name!' That, in a word, is *overselling*. But if I go to a publisher and say, 'I have an idea, and I think it's a very powerful idea, and you'll have to determine as a publisher whether you think it's viable'—well, that's plenty. I don't have to oversell it. I believe in the idea, and the publisher knows it.

"When you put on too much make-up, Mushki, you're overselling yourself. And you of all people don't need to sell yourself! You have something many others girls don't have, real feminine dignity, and it shows in every aspect of your demeanor: in your soft, gentle disposition, in your extraordinary maturity. Don't become hard. Don't become a line. Be careful always not to become one of those people for whom the external is more important than the internal, for whom form is greater than substance. You already have tremendous strength. It's the men who often fight about money, power, the size of their homes, the types of cars they drive—because those are the weapons they use to sell themselves. But if you're a strong person on the inside you don't have to show fake strength on the outside. You of all people don't need to this. You are already beautiful naturally."

"So I should remove it?"

"No. You can use make-up on special occasions, like the Sabbath, but use it sparingly. Make-up should be about highlighting beauty, not about masking ugliness, not about salesmanship."

I also talk to my eldest son about femininity, for the two reasons I mentioned earlier: I want him to honor women, and I want him to nurture his own femininity. He's a really good boy, and he's already very nurturing, largely because he's been raised around girls—he has five sisters—and because his mother is a very feminine, very nurturing woman. In short, he's already quite comfortable with that side of himself, and I know it will make him a better man.

Now, as I said, he's a really good boy, almost a *perfect* boy, and that is why I was so shocked by the story I am about to tell you. I came home one night, shortly after ten, and I found him on one of those Internet chat rooms with several kids from his class at school. He was eleven years old at the time. I watched for a few moments, and I saw that it was all boys, since my son goes to an Orthodox, boys-only day school, but suddenly a girl came online, someone they knew from the neighborhood, and almost immediately one of the other boys referred to her as a "bitch." I couldn't believe it. At a religious day school, and at that age? I took my son aside and confronted him. "How can you be friends with a boy who has no respect for girls?" I asked him. "What kind of man would call a girl such a thing? The most important thing in your upbringing is to grow up to be a gentleman, a *mensch*. And a gentleman is discerned above all else by how he treats girls, by how he treats women. When you get to school tomorrow, Mendy, I want you to confront that boy. I want you to tell him, 'I have five sisters. You don't talk about a girl like that. That is a disgusting word and I don't like it and you should never use it.'"

I didn't stop there—I wanted my son to really understand why this was so important to me: "Virtually every divorce that I have seen involves a husband who doesn't sufficiently cherish the feminine," I told him. "These husbands come home and they take for granted all that their wives do for them. As a result, the wife becomes harder toward the man she once loved. That's what happened with my parents, as you know, *your* grandparents. Saba came from a very poor background, and he worked very hard to make money. But he wasn't around often enough. And by the time he came home, he was so beat up from work that he often had very little affection to share. He didn't make Grandma feel cherished. So she steeled herself against his hardness until she stopped feeling for him, and the family drifted apart. So this is really close to home for you, and I am disturbed that you would allow this boy to refer to a girl as a 'bitch.' That's tantamount to condoning it. You have been taught to respect women—even to be in awe of them. How is it possible that you didn't protest the use of that expression?"

My son fought back tears and apologized, saying he'd never let it happen again.

"You must always respect women," I continued. "And part of that is to inspire your friends to do the same. There should be no room in your life for boys who put girls down and call them names."

Some parents might say I overreacted, but I don't believe so. I spoke to my son calmly but sternly. I had no rancor in my voice, and I spoke to him from the heart. But I was going to get my message through. I was raised by a single mother who did everything for her five kids. I *am* in awe of women, and I will raise my sons to feel the same. The conversation was designed to underscore something my son already knew, because we talked of it often: *In our home we honor the feminine.*

And we respect the feminine *in every form.* I tell you this because I am thinking of another story, a very personal story. I have a brother who is gay—and to be Orthodox, Jewish, *and* gay is very challenging, believe me. I am very close to my brother, as are my kids, and I often talk to them about their uncle. I see my brother as a highly evolved human being, a man with a golden heart. I have often said, a little facetiously, admittedly, that the perfect man is a gay man who is attracted to women. Still, there's a bit of truth to it. I believe that the perfect man is a nurturer who isn't afraid to be a nurturer, and my brother is eminently qualified for the job. While I am completely accepting of my brother, I have to admit that I lament that he never married and had kids because I believe he would be a wonderful father— a much better father than I am, in fact. Even as children, while I was off doing all the manly things—playing sports, running around, getting into trouble—I could see that my brother was already superior to me in his emotional development. He was only a year older, but he was sensitive, well-rounded, tender, and inordinately concerned with our mother's welfare.

> ᴄ๏
>
> THE PERFECT MAN IS A
> NURTURER WHO ISN'T
> AFRAID TO BE A NURTURER.
>
> ᴄ๏

In later years, I worked at becoming more like him—at becoming a more feminine and emotionally available man. Or, as I've taken to calling it, a *Circle Man*. I want to be domesticated, I want to be less linear and more pliable, less goal-oriented and more means-oriented. I want to be able to speak to my wife about the things that weigh on my heart, and I want to learn to cut through all of the emotional baggage that so often saddles so many men, myself included.

This reminds me of another story: Some months ago, a man came to see me for counseling. He had recently switched jobs, and things weren't going well, and he was having a very tough time. So I asked him, "Do you talk to your wife about these things?" And he said, "No." And I asked, "Why not?" And he just shut down—I could literally see him shutting down. "Because I don't want to," he said. "I'm just not comfortable with it."

I shared this story with my children and expounded further: "Too many men these days have the same problem. They refuse to get in touch with the softer side of themselves, their feminine side. They won't talk about pain, or about feelings of failure, or about the things that really count, because they are afraid to appear weak. They think people will look at them as failures. So they hold everything inside, giving their emotions no outlet, and their feelings gnaw away at them and destroy their lives. Often, the first thing to be destroyed is the marriage. These men do not allow their wives to fulfill their roles as nurturers. A woman cannot nurture a man who shows no emotion. And a man who is unable to show emotion has little understanding of the feminine, both without and within."

This reminded me of yet another story, one that actually illustrates how far such a man might fall, and I shared that with them, too. "I know a man, I'll call him George, whose wife informed him, suddenly and unexpectedly, that she wanted to separate. The man was absolutely shattered. The marriage had not been perfect, and he did not pretend to have been a perfect husband, but he had a two-year-old son, and he didn't want to put him through a divorce. In the interest of making things easier on his wife and son, and in the hopes that they might reconcile, George immediately offered to move into a nearby hotel. He had a few good friends, of course, and they would phone him from time to time, and take him to lunch or to dinner and let him talk, which is what he most needed at that difficult time. But one of the friends—let's call him Mark—never phoned, and this was odd and disturbing because Mark had been very much part of George's life. Mark was married, and he had a little girl the same age as George's son, and they had often socialized, sometime with their wives, and sometimes as dads out for a Sunday stroll with their toddlers.

"Weeks went by, and George continued to live in the hotel, trying to repair his marriage, which was beginning to look less and less likely, and still Mark didn't call. Finally, after an entire month, the phone rang in George's hotel room. It was Mark, at long last. He said a few noncommittal things—'tough times,' 'hang in,'—and George patiently heard him out. When Mark was finally done stumbling along, saying things he didn't actually seem to feel, it was George's turn to talk. 'Listen, Mark, I want to tell you that I am very glad you finally called me,' he told his old friend. 'It is good to hear your voice. But I must also say that I expected to hear from you a long time ago, and I have been very hurt. My life has been turned upside down by this, and I'm living in one small room in a hotel, and I miss my kid so badly that I'm always on the point of tears. I thought that you of all people would have reached out to me.'

"And Mark took a moment, then said, 'George, you sound like a girl.'

"Isn't that terrible? Mark had not only failed to reach out to his injured friend, but had berated and insulted him for expressing his true feelings, for being 'weak enough' to experience pain.

"What kind of man does that, and to a close friend? Well, I will tell you what kind of man: *a man who has never developed a gift for nurturing.* That, to me, is a man who has lost something very precious. He has not only purged himself of his nurturing instincts, but he actually *mocks* a man who has them. Imagine: We are creating a world where a man is berated for *feeling!*"

It is hard for me to understand that type of hardness. To me, the feminine is something to be revered. When I was in Yeshiva in Israel, studying to become a rabbi, I had no exposure to girls. It was forbidden. All we did was study. The very idea that girls existed was enchanting to us rabbinical students. We looked at women not as objects of lust, but as awe-inspiring creatures. To us, a woman was like an angel. I couldn't wait to meet a woman and marry her and live with her at my side. To have a wife of my own—whoa! The very thought was amazing.

Before long, this came to pass. I met a wonderful woman, and I asked her to marry me, and she agreed to become my bride. When I looked at her, I knew that I would never even *glance* at another woman. I didn't need to; I had found the fairest woman of them all.

The morning after our wedding, I ran out to the store to buy a camera. We were looking forward to the traditional seven days of celebration, and I wanted to record every moment of those happy days. When I arrived at the shopping mall, I found an electronics store, and the young woman who sold the camera to me was not only very helpful, but very pretty. I went back to the house, devastated. How was it possible that I, a married man, could still find other women attractive? I couldn't believe it! How could I even notice? Was love really so imperfect?

When I got home, I apologized to my wife and hung my head in shame. "Debbie," I said. "You married a scoundrel." I told her the story about the young lady, with my head hung low. "I'm such a jerk," I said. But Debbie was laughing. "Take it easy and stop being so ridiculous. Everything's fine."

My wife may have been dismissive of my guilt, but I spent years thinking about the seemingly imperfect nature of love. Why is that we are never immune to the attraction posed by strangers, even when we are deeply and happily in love? And it occurred to me that love *has to* operate in this manner. The fact that a husband is attracted to other women is partly what makes love so special—the idea that he comes home every night and *chooses his wife anew*. Love is not meant to be static. It is designed to be constantly refreshed. Years later, I told Debbie: "You know, that morning after my visit to the camera shop? I now understand it. Our commitment to each other is not something static or staid, but a love that is constantly being rejuvenated and renewed."

What does a woman want from her husband? Love? Perhaps, but not exactly. She was loved by her parents, after all, and as she grew up she wanted something more. What a woman really wants is *to be chosen*. The main thing a husband can do for his wife, the one thing her parents could never do for her, is to *choose* her—to turn her into the chosen one. This is how a man honors a woman, and there is no greater honor. Even the Bible sees it this way. It says that God's love for the Jewish people is manifest in Him not just through His love for them, but for having *chosen* them. And the Jews have been the chosen people ever since.

That is how the line and the circle complement each other, how they function as a whole. And, I find this very interesting, in fulfilling their assigned roles men and women are not all that dissimilar from the system of "checks and balances" that makes this country work. It is the very system that God instituted in his infinite wisdom: pairing the feminine with the masculine, the line with the circle.

I tell my children, "Women need men. Men have raw energy. They can chop down whole forests, drain swamps, and build cities. Male aggression is necessary, but unchecked it becomes brutal. The feminine neutralizes masculine aggression and makes it more refined. And in neutralizing the male tendency toward aggression, it paves the way for transcendence. Women are naturally more spiritual than men. They have a more natural spiritual instinct. A woman should never lose sight of that within herself, and a man should never forget that he is ennobled through his devotion to a woman."

I tell them, "Women are changing the world. They are trying to do away with aggression and warfare and *manhood*. Women are bringing about a quantum shift in our perception of heroism. Nowadays, many of our great heroes aren't masculine at all. Men like Mahatma Gandhi and Nelson Mandela are not manly in the traditional sense, but they are the kind of men we need—men who beat their swords into ploughshares, men who forgive rather than fight. Thanks to the influence of women, we have finally learned to respect and honor those types of men. In the old days, we only respected emperors who conquered and swallowed other nations, but those men are now hunted down and put in jail. This is what I call the *feminization of history*. History begins with the masculine and moves toward the feminine. And that's messianic progress."

All of us, men and women alike, should be nurturing our feminine sides. That is the future. When we fail to do this, we masculinize the feminine. Case in point: Those hardened sisters in Connecticut—sweet girls all, but they had lost their desire to be nurturers.

Women are healers. When men have no feminine influence, their aggression has nothing to check it. If you don't believe me, take a look around you: Wherever women have a strong voice in a culture or society, that culture is invariably more peaceful. Norway, for example, exports peace, and they have a higher rate of women in politics than any other country in the world. Women are natural peacemakers. It is the wife who brings peacefulness into the home. It is the wife who cures the brokenness of the American male. She's the one who says, "You're not going to be special by making more money. You're going to be special by being a father, by being domesticated, and by loving your children and reading them bedtime stories."

When men don't allow their wives to influence them, expect disharmony. The line must

> ❧
>
> WOMEN ARE BRINGING ABOUT A QUANTUM SHIFT IN OUR PERCEPTION OF HEROISM.
>
> ❧

become less rigid. This is what happened in my parents' home. My father is a great man and I can't even begin to tell you how much I admire him, but he didn't allow himself to be softened by the woman at his side. He was an immigrant in this country, determined to provide for his family, and that determination took over his entire life. He succeeded, beyond even his own expectations, but his marriage fell apart in the process.

Alas, we men are often slaves to the thymotic urge: We need to be recognized for our achievements. Nobody makes movies about men who help their kids with their homework, or who take out the garbage without being asked. As a result, we measure success by our professional standing and the money in our bank accounts, not by the quality of our relationships.

Sadly, families tend to pass their flaws along from generation to generation. Two of my sisters, for example, whom I love with all my heart and to whom I am immensely devoted, are divorced. My older sister, Sara, struggled for a long time with her son, Jordan, who as a confused and angry teenager seemed intent on *dis*honoring his mother. It seemed, then, that one of the family flaws was being passed on to him.

Jordan went through a rebellious period and fought with his mother in ugly ways. Oddly enough, even as the fights escalated, Jordan was becoming more religious. It was hard to understand. He was going more often to the synagogue, going to more Jewish classes, and observing the holy laws. But he was behaving in increasingly disrespectful ways toward his mother. It wasn't that he didn't love her. On the contrary, he adored his mother and always remained close to her—and in fact had always been a mama's boy (which I say as a compliment). But my sister didn't want him hanging out with the wrong crowd or doing things that would be injurious to him, and Jordan began to chafe against the rules.

One day, after having witnessed another painful altercation, I took Jordan aside. "Look," I said, "your mother is raising six children as a single mother. She works very hard to pay the bills. There is nothing she doesn't do for you. And the way you speak to her is shocking. On the other hand, you genuinely want to become more religious. You're studying, praying, going to synagogue more frequently. I salute that and I know you love your mother. I also know that you took your parents' divorce harder than you probably know, and you are struggling to deal with your anger. So at some point you have to ask yourself: *Is this how I want to treat my mother? Is this how I treat women? Is this the kind of person I want to be—a man who dishonors women?*

"Do you want to be another religious faker? I don't understand you. How is it possible that you can speak to God so warmly, then turn around and call your mother—the mother you love and adore—ugly names? Your job is to ease your mother's burden, Jordan. I was a child of divorce, so I know and understand: My mother had to raise five kids on her own. She worked as a bank teller during the day, five days a week, and as a check-out clerk at a supermarket at night, so that we could eat—so that there would be clothes on our backs. My siblings and I knew that our role was *to ease our mother's burden,* and we tried to be good kids. Are you listening to me?"

"Yes," he said.

"There are many things in my life that I've done wrong, and they still pain me," I went on. "But the things that really pain me the most are not the sins of commission, the bad things I've done, but the sins of omission—the good things I failed to do. One of the greatest failures in my life was that I didn't provide *greater* comfort to my mother; that I didn't do more; that we kids often left the house a mess and fought among ourselves and let our tempers get out of control. I wish I had had the ability to say to myself, 'Enough! Enough! Here is a woman with five kids and two jobs, putting her kids through a Jewish day school, struggling to make ends meet. Stop adding to her misery!' That pains me more than I can tell you, but even at my worst moments I never spoke to her the way you speak to your mother, because even then I still knew enough to *honor* her."

I left, thinking I had gotten through to him, but before long I again heard from my sister, who said she thought that Jordan had been introduced to marijuana by one of his friends. She forbade him from seeing this boy, but he refused to listen, so in despair she called up the boy's parents and told them: "Your son and my son are smoking pot together. They are a bad influence on each other and I think we should keep them apart." The parents had no idea that their son was smoking pot, but they looked into it and found out that my sister was right, and they confronted their son. The next night, that boy phoned my sister's house, and he called her every ugly name in the book: *bitch, whore, slut*. He was furious at her for telling his parents.

When I found out, I was so angry that I wanted to slap this fifteen-year-old across the face.

How dare he speak to my sister like that, the little punk? I had never heard anything so outrageous! Instead, I took hold of my anger and went to see my nephew. "You see what happens, Jordan?" I said. "Do you know why that boy spoke to your mother in that ugly way?"

"Why?"

"*Because he saw you speaking to her like that*," I said. "How can this be, Jordan? How can it not cause you pain, knowing that a friend of yours spoke to your mother in that horrendous manner? You are a good person, Jordan, so you need to confront this so-called friend. 'Until you call my mother and apologize,' you need to tell him, 'I will not speak to you ever again.'

"Don't you see? Disrespect breeds disrespect. And it will pain you forever because you are becoming something you never wanted to be. Did you ever want to be the kind of man who causes his mother pain? Men have to honor and respect women, and that goes tenfold for your own mother."

Jordan hung his head and listened in silence.

"I will tell you something, Jordan. I am a rabbi and a counselor, and I know something about pain. And I want you to think about this: I have seen people's lives fall apart after a parent has died because they regret all the things that went unsaid and that now can never be said. All the love that must now remain unexpressed—it's heart wrenching. The death of a parent is one of the great triggers for a mid-life crisis. A man loses a parent and it crushes him. All the sins of omission—all the things he could have done differently—all the things he can never undo. There's no going back. And it poisons his entire life. Do you understand what I'm telling you?"

"Yes."

"Your mother will survive, Jordan, but your goodness won't. If you don't correct your behavior, you will become a man who doesn't sufficiently respect women, who hardens the softer sex because of his aggression toward them. That type of man risks depriving himself of one of life's great blessings— namely, finding feminine warmth and comfort."

I knew he was hurting. The father and the mother are the sun and the moon to a child. The father brings life to the home, which illuminates the mother and makes her feel cherished and loved. From that light, together, they produce the joy in the home. Jordan's pain explained his behavior, but it didn't excuse it.

Being an uncle has some precious rewards that even fatherhood lacks, and I have often tried to take Jordan under my wing. To his credit, he turned his entire life around, became an outstanding son to his mother, stopped smoking pot, and went to an advanced religious seminary in Jerusalem. He is currently going to university in New York where he is a leader among his peers, and spends most weekends with me and my family. Jordan's presence in my life is one of my greatest joys and I look up to him tremendously for the courage he showed in turning himself around. He is authentically religious and shows everyone he meets an inordinate amount of respect. Jordan often thanks me for having inspired him, but I tell him I was only a small part of it. "You were responding to your own inner voice," I explain. "Your motivation came from within."

I often talk to my kids about my parents' divorce because they are curious, and because they ask, and because by not answering I risk making them less curious—and, as I've said, I can't sufficiently stress the importance of intellectual curiosity.

Every time a marriage falls apart—whether it's a relative, a family friend, or a neighbor—my kids ask me about that, too, because I'm a marital counselor, and because they think I might have some of the answers. My daughter once asked, "What does irreconcilable differences mean?" And I told her, "What it means is this: Every human being is different from every other human being. But people find each other, and the love and attraction is greater than the differences. Your love for that person helped you overcome whatever differences existed.

"Irreconcilable differences simply means that the attraction these two people once shared has been lost, and all they are left with are the differences. And that's what happens to many marriages. People stop choosing their partner."

I spoke earlier about Moses, and how he taught the Jewish people that feelings of emptiness come from within. And I use that in marital counseling all the time. When a husband tells me that he is no longer attracted to his wife, I say to him, "Your wife is still beautiful. The emptiness is in you.

> ❧
>
> WHEN A HUSBAND TELLS ME THAT HE IS NO LONGER ATTRACTED TO HIS WIFE, I SAY TO HIM, "YOUR WIFE IS STILL BEAUTIFUL. THE EMPTINESS IS IN YOU."
>
> ❧

You have lost the capacity to be stimulated by the everyday. You now need a young bombshell. You now need to buy a Porsche. You're a man who is addicted to bells and whistles, and you'll get bored with them, too, because the problem—the emptiness—is in you, not in your wife." In short, this man has lost the capacity to honor the feminine. He can only honor a cheap, flimsy version of the feminine.

King Solomon, the wisest of all men, wrote: "See life with the woman you love."

This is what I tell my children: "A man must always honor the women in his life, and both men and women must honor the sacred feminine within each of them. For only through cherishing the feminine do we create a warm and wondrous world."

6

FORGIVENESS

A CHILD NEEDS TO UNDERSTAND ONE OF THE
BASIC TRUTHS ABOUT FORGIVENESS:
WHEN WE FORGIVE, WE ARE DOING IT
FIRST AND FOREMOST FOR OURSELVES.

A child who doesn't learn how to forgive is a child who lives in a prison of his own making. Resentment, hostility, and anger have turned him into a prisoner. That child needs to understand one of the basic truths about forgiveness: *When we forgive, we are doing it first and foremost for ourselves.*

Earlier, I spoke of a family in Connecticut—several children from two broken homes, struggling to adjust to life under one roof. The eldest daughter was off in college, and she was doing fine, and the other children were dealing with the situation as well as they could, but the sixteen-year-old girl was completely unforgiving. When I tried to talk to her about how she hoped to address the issue, she was dismissive. "I don't care about any of that. All I care about is being successful. *I don't want to need anyone.*"

Later, I spoke to my children about my interactions with her. "She was only sixteen years old, but she had the cynicism of a forty-year-old. Her heart was becoming hard. I told her, 'The best you can do is to forgive your parents for the mistakes they made and move forward. To be angry and unforgiving only makes you hold onto your pain. Anger is a terrible thing. It robs a home of peace. It destroys marriages. It ruins lives. And it is threatening to ruin your life.'

"I want you kids to know that if any of you are ever angry with me, for whatever reason, you need to talk to me about it. If I make mistakes with you, and I'm sure I do, I want an opportunity to apologize, and to address those mistakes."

As my children know, one of the central themes of Judaism is that you can't be fully human if you don't learn how to forgive. But children today seem to be angrier and more unforgiving than at any other time in history. Indeed, anger has become such a pervasive part of growing up in this day and age that it seems to be an accepted rite of passage. This, to me, is a catastrophe. If your child is angry with you, you need to deal with it. If you've done something to make your child angry, you need to face it. And even if your child only *thinks* he's angry with you, you need to figure that out, too. You mustn't let anger fester. Anger is a destroyer of lives. Volatility seems to be the standard nowadays, the happy home a thing of the past—something from an earlier, gentler era. You don't see a single show on television today that tries to sell the idea of a "happy marriage," and that's probably because no one would buy it. We make fun of *The Brady Bunch*, who were a happy, smiling, communicative family! That's ridiculous!

I myself come from a broken home, so I understand what it does to people, and it has made me cautious about my own role as a father. I feel it is my responsibility to absorb the pain and chaos I was raised in, to figure out how to filter it through my system and heal the wounds so that I don't pass it on to my own children. My great fear is that I will do to them what

> ANGER HAS BECOME SUCH A PERVASIVE PART OF GROWING UP IN THIS DAY AND AGE THAT IT SEEMS TO BE AN ACCEPTED RITE OF PASSAGE. THIS, TO ME, IS A CATASTROPHE.

was done to me. One cannot raise children in chaos and volatility. They have to see an example of loving parents and a well-ordered home.

Do I always succeed? No, far from it. My father, as I said earlier, is a great man, but a complicated one, and I've inherited some of those complications. I sometimes yell at my kids, less so since becoming host of *Shalom in the Home*—which in many ways really opened my eyes to the amount of yelling in the average household, and to its horrendously destructive nature.

Still, there was a time when my daughter Chana seemed a little bit afraid of my volatility. I noticed this, and I tried to control even the most sporadic outburst, and whenever I failed to control it I would apologize to her, but I was apologizing so frequently that my eldest child Mushki became increasingly cynical. "Tatty, what's the point of apologizing when you know you're going to do the exact same thing again?"

She was right. A few nights later, I made this the subject of our dinnertime conversation. "Look," I said, "your father, what makes him, hopefully, a decent man, is that he wrestles with his mistakes, he struggles to be a better man. But he is not a perfect man. Your father is flawed, and he is full of contradictions. Try as I might, I don't always succeed in doing what I know to be the right thing."

Last summer, I did a radio tour with my family across the American South, broadcasting from a different city five days a week. We covered 6,000 miles in our RV. There were nine of us, plus two friends, inside the vehicle, and—believe me—it can get on your nerves in no time at all. I found myself speaking harshly to the kids. "Come on! I'm tired. I've been driving all day! Move, move, move!" Needless to say, this created a nervous environment.

One night, a beautiful Friday night, we were having our Shabbat dinner out in the woods, next to the RV, listening to the chirping of the crickets. Toward the end of dinner, I asked for everyone's attention. "Listen," I said. "I have something to say for about twenty minutes, after which I'm going to go completely silent and give you guys forty minutes to respond. We're going to spend one hour on this. One full hour. You can say whatever you want in response. No holds barred. Just be respectful, that's all I ask.

"I want to begin by saying that you guys are the light of my life. You guys bring me so much joy, and one of the reasons I love going on these road trips with you is that I get to spend so much time with you in close quarters. I know I tend to get busy at home, and sometimes I don't focus on all you guys as much as I would like, and going on these trips together makes me feel very close to all of you. Still, even when we're away, I sometimes feel that we're not as close as I'd like us to be, and I know that this is because I have hurt you at times. I've yelled at you, sometimes fairly, sometimes unfairly, but even when it was fair it wasn't fair. There is no excuse, ever, for a parent to lose his temper, no excuse to raise one's voice. I realize that at such times I have failed you as a father, and I'm asking you to forgive me.

"I am also asking you to please try to understand that what I want most in my life is to give you *what I wasn't given*. This is not about stuff, this is not about an iPod or a big house, but about the gift of peace. I want you to grow up in a home where there is minimal volatility, a place where you can internalize peace. If I can do that, you will be able to handle whatever life throws at you in the years to come. Each of you will be like a hurricane: strong winds on the outside, with peace at your center. No amount of volatility will unnerve you."

I then turned to my second daughter: "Chana, I know there are times when you are distant from me because you feel I have hurt you with unpredictable moods," I said. "And I'm asking you to forgive me because you deserve a soft, warm father who shows consistency. Nothing hurts me more than the thought that I could have hurt you, and that as a result you are slightly more distant from me. I love you with all my heart and I ask you to forgive me."

By that point, Chana was quietly sobbing, which was unusual—she is not a girl who shows a lot of vulnerability—and the other kids were trying to interrupt: "Stop, Tatty! You're being way too hard on yourself! You're a great father!" And I said, "*No.* I'm going to speak for twenty minutes, and then you'll speak."

And I really spoke from the heart. I said, "I'm trying my best to ensure that whatever shortcomings exist in the generational life of our family are going to stop with me. I'm trying very hard to heal myself so that you guys will never suffer any pain—at least from me. I can't control what others will do to you, but I can certainly control what I do, and that is my solemn promise to you, here, tonight: that I will work harder to always be the best father I can be."

It was quite eerie. All you could hear was the crickets chirping, me talking, and Chana quietly sobbing. But I was happy. The subject of forgiveness is critical, and the evening already felt magical to me. I knew I was getting through to them just by looking at their faces. I know children, my own and many others. And I know that they will seldom talk to you about the things that hurt them. They'll talk about getting shortchanged when the chocolate cake comes around, but they won't talk about the truly important feelings. They internalize those; they get angry; they distance themselves from you and often even from the rest of the family. I didn't want that happening in our home.

"I have seen children become hard because they are in pain and because no one acknowledges the pain," I said. "This is perhaps because they are afraid to let others see it, afraid that their pain and anger will only make things worse, or that it is somehow 'wrong.' But this

&

CHILDREN WILL SELDOM
TALK TO YOU ABOUT THE
THINGS THAT HURT THEM.

&

should never happen in our home. Mistakes will be made, certainly, by all of us, but when we cause each other pain we need to talk about it. If I hurt you and I am unaware of it, I can't address it. By allowing me to see my mistakes, you will be helping me become a better man."

When I was finished, everyone became very silent, and I said, "Okay. Now it's your turn. Tell me the things that I've done that are wrong. All I ask is that you do it respectfully because I, also, can be wounded."

So for forty minutes we went around the table, one by one, with me as the moderator, and each child told me what he or she was thinking. Not surprisingly, the younger ones had no real complaints. But the older kids spoke their minds, and they had four basic grievances: first and foremost, that I shouted, which I promised to stop. I was raised with yelling, I explained, and I was unwittingly bequeathing that to my children, but that was no excuse. My yelling was unacceptable, and I would redouble my efforts to address the problem.

The next complaint came from my son Mendy, who said I didn't always listen. He's a big reader and a big fan of information, like his father, but I don't always have time to hear about Abraham Lincoln's various nicknames or the last time the Olympics were held in Athens, so I sometimes tune him out. That really bothered him, and I thanked him for telling me because until we spoke about it that evening I didn't realize how much he was being hurt by what he perceived as my indifference.

The next complaint came from Sterni, my thirteen-year-old, who hates the fact that I smoke an occasional cigar. I explained that I do it to relax, especially when I'm writing, but I agreed that it was a disgusting habit and assured her that I would make an effort to phase it out.

The final and most startling grievance came from my eldest daughter Mushki, who said that I sometimes appeared disrespectful of my own wife. She gave me some examples, doing her best to mimic my tone. "You'll say something like, 'Debbie, what do you mean you didn't take care of that! You knew I needed it *today*! I thought you knew that!'" In listening to Mushki, and in being made aware of how I sounded to her and to the rest of my family, I realized I would need to work on two things—tone and delivery—and I assured them I would do so. But I have to admit that it was the most hurtful criticism because I worship my wife, and I thought this was evident to my kids. I want them to believe in love, and I want them to know that a marriage can really work, despite all the modern evidence to the contrary, so I have been working very hard on that.

That was a life-changing evening for me, and I don't use those words lightly. In seeking forgiveness from my children, they taught me a great deal about the things I needed to address in myself, and they gave me a chance to work on personal shortcomings that were clearly having an effect on my entire family.

Fast-forward three months to Yom Kippur evening at our home. The evening is all about forgiveness and atonement, and it is considered the holiest night of the Jewish year. We prayed the holy *kol nidre* service, and when it was over I took my wife and kids into the study so we could share a few moments of privacy. "As you know," I began, "the custom on Yom Kippur is that God can forgive you for the things that you've done against God—blasphemy, desecrating the Sabbath, and so on—but He cannot forgive you for any pain you've caused other people. Even God can't grant forgiveness for harming others. You have to seek that directly from the injured party, and only they can bestow it. So I want to ask forgiveness from all of you if I've hurt you in any way."

> ONE MUSTN'T ALWAYS JUDGE PEOPLE BY WHAT THEY DO, BUT BY HOW FAR THEY'VE COME. NOT BY THE DESTINATION, BUT BY THE JOURNEY.

I impressed on them that one mustn't always judge people by what they do, but by *how far they've come*. Not by the destination, but by the journey.

"Your father, unlike you, thank God, was raised in a very challenging environment," I went on. "I saw nothing but fighting. We even saw the police at our house. To this day, more than thirty years after the divorce, my parents do not speak to each other. I internalized a lot of that, but I have tried hard to get it out of my system. I know I'm not there yet, but I will always try to do better."

The reason forgiveness is so important, and the reason it is such a central theme of Judaism, is, as I said, because *we believe that you can't be fully human if you don't forgive.* This is what I was trying to impress on my children through these conversations.

I am not the only person in our home who makes mistakes, but I am responsible for the way those mistakes are handled. When one of my children does something wrong, we deal with it, forgive him or her, and move on. But forgiveness goes much deeper, and I needed them to understand that. Part of it is about making the offender feel better, and about reestablishing the connection, but the main reason we do it is for *us*—so that we don't let it poison our hearts and turn them to stone.

"An unforgiving heart is a heavy heart," I tell my children. "When you don't forgive someone, you become bitter, and that feeling festers, affecting you more than it affects them. When you forgive, the one you are truly freeing is yourself."

7

FAMILY AND TRADITION

FAR TOO MANY FAMILIES NOWADAYS
LIVE TOGETHER AS STRANGERS.

T he successful man or woman is the man or woman who is first and foremost successful with his or her family.

When I was growing up, my father, due to my parents' divorce, was seldom present to guide me, and I had to do most things on my own. As a result, I have worked doubly hard at being a real influence in the lives of my children.

In my other life, my professional life, I often feel like I'm coming up short. *My last book sold, but it didn't sell as well as I had hoped. The television show is shaping up, but will anyone tune in? I delivered a speech tonight and everyone told me it was wonderful, but who knows if they meant it?* In short, I'm just like everyone else, with my fair share of insecurities. But as a father, miraculously enough, I sometimes feel as if I'm actually getting through to my kids.

Let me give you an example. My eldest daughter Mushki is a senior in high school, and she's been applying to colleges. Being a curious father, as well as a writer, I asked her if I could take a look at her essays. She didn't write the essays thinking I would look at them, so she didn't write them for me, but she was happy to let me take a look. After reading them, I went upstairs to my wife, and said, "You know what? I might not be the big loser I think I am. I might actually be a success."

"What do you mean?" she asked.

Both of Mushki's essays were based on themes I've been drilling into the kids for years. One was about the importance of bestowing dignity, and the other one was about the primacy of family. "I never knew if she was really hearing me," I told my wife. "But I'm amazed at the impact I've actually had on my kids, thank God."

The lesson here is simple: Even when you're not sure you're getting through to your kids, you're getting through to them. If you make an investment, you will reap the reward. That's what makes these conversations so important. Success is never immediate, and sometimes it's nowhere in evidence, but talking to your kids really works.

And, no, it's not easy—children become increasingly uncommunicative as they grow up—but it's your responsibility as a parent to see that your family is a family in the truest sense of the word. I think a little mandatory "togetherness" can go a very long way, and a number of recent studies actually back this up. Families who share meals on a regular basis, and make an effort to communicate while they're at it, have children who perform better in school, exhibit more self-esteem, and feel as if they are more in control of their lives.

> SUCCESS IS NEVER IMMEDIATE, AND SOMETIMES IT'S NOWHERE IN EVIDENCE, BUT TALKING TO YOUR KIDS REALLY WORKS.

In our family, we try to have dinner together every night. More than any other activity, family dinners help define a family. This is *family* time. No phones, no doorbells, no interruptions. We are all part of each other's lives, and I want my children to know it and appreciate it.

Taking your son to a Little League game is also important, because every minute you spend with your children is a gift, but that doesn't define the family. A family is a group of people who live together, and far too many families nowadays live together as strangers. That is why we must make a concerted effort to be a family in the truest sense of the word, and why family dinners are an essential first step. Aside from the obvious togetherness, it provides the perfect arena for these important conversations. Everyone is acknowledged, everyone is part of the conversation, and everyone is listening (whether they want to or not).

In our home, we don't struggle to make time to talk to each other because it is built into our lives. And the kids look forward to it. They don't whine and roll their eyes, as they do in some homes. They come to the table to talk, listen, and share. In the course of dinner, everyone is heard, everyone is *validated*.

We do plenty of other things to promote our sense of family. Several nights a week, for example, I'll take fifteen minutes to read from the Bible, with my family gathered around me, and I'll always make an effort to find something germane. If two boys got into a fight in the school yard that day, and my son happened to mention it at the dinner table, I'll look for a Biblical passage that speaks to issues of violence and vengeance. Not that hard, is it?

When parents call to ask if I can counsel their children, I always tell them that I would be happy to, but only after an initial consultation with the parents. When they show up, regardless of the nature of the problem at home, I always try to determine how much time the family spends together as a family. It's usually very little, and the story is always the same: *We are busy people; the kids are overscheduled; there simply aren't enough hours in the day.* Unfortunately, I can't accept that as an answer. After all, we all live and operate in the same world. These parents are usually struggling with the *urgent* versus the *important*, a concept I dealt with in my book, *Judaism for Everyone.* So I tell them: "Let's say you are reading your son a bedtime story, and your cell phone rings, and in your heart you know it's important to read to your son—you are connecting with him, teaching him to love books—but this call is from the office, and you know it's urgent. What do you do? You take the call, right? After all, your son will still be there when you're done with the call, waiting for you to pick up where you left off, but the call will be gone. Sound reasoning, but very unhealthy, because this becomes the pattern. Ballet recital? Well, this conference is going to run long, and I'm sure my little girl will understand. Family dinner? My boss wants me to entertain the new clients, and we really need this account.

"Before long, the urgent takes over, and the important becomes less and less important, until the child himself feels unimportant," I tell the parent. "That's why you're having problems with your child. He doesn't need me; he needs *you.*"

Parents tell me they don't know where to begin, but this is not an excuse, either. One might begin the moment the child comes home from school. "Drop everything and spend the next five minutes fully focused on him," I suggest.

> ∞
>
> AS A PARENT, YOU'VE
> EARNED THE RIGHT TO
> HAVE A RELATIONSHIP WITH
> YOUR CHILD.
>
> ∞

"What he did that day, how much homework he has, what's on the agenda for tomorrow, and so on. It's really not that complicated. It's about making conversation, even if you have to pull it out of him. In time, it will become part of family life, and the family will be stronger for it.

"And don't waiver," I tell the parents. "Never forget that, as a parent, you've earned the right to have a relationship with your child. Beyond that, you also have the right to expect a little gratitude and appreciation."

I often talk to my children about this very topic: "Let me ask you this: Why do you think God included the edict that you must honor your parents in the Ten Commandments? Why is that one of the cardinal rules of morality? Why is that up there with 'Do not kill'? Isn't it puzzling? That this business about 'honoring your mother and father' is a key element of morality?

"Well, I'll tell you why it's there: It's a form of gratitude. Your parents gave you life. They fed you when you were helpless; they loved you when you were alone; they cared for you and nurtured you when you were at your most vulnerable point. God is saying, *At the very least, you must honor your parents for everything they have done for you.* It is the ultimate evocation of gratitude. You don't have to fawn over your parents, but God expects you to be human enough to be touched by their love.

"Your responsibility as kids, then, is to show your parents, always, that their efforts do not go unnoticed."

The obligation, as you may have noticed, is to *honor* one's parents, not to love them. This is because the Bible in its wisdom understands that a child may not always feel love for his parents. There will be times when he is angry, frustrated, bitter, even hostile. Let's face it. Parents do make a lot of mistakes in rearing their children, and often the child feels wronged. But this doesn't give him the right to treat his parents with disrespect.

You need to talk to your children about this, and regular, dinnertime conversations are a good start, but they are only a start. Regular conversation needs to become part of the family *routine;* beyond that, we get into questions of *tradition.*

In my family, as is obvious, the traditions are those of Orthodox Judaism. We read the Bible, observe the Sabbath and Biblical festivals, go to synagogue, keep a strictly kosher home, and live by the Jewish values of community, charity, hospitality, and humanity. I teach my children everything I can about their heritage because I want them to remember who they are and where their people came from, but I also insist that they not become insular or exclusionary. "As long as a set of beliefs leads to a righteous, generous, and moral life, it is holy and Godly," I tell them.

To me, religion is about identity, and identity speaks to character. The child who knows himself—be it through routine, tradition, or faith—is strengthened by that self-knowledge.

It goes without saying, of course, that every family has its own history, and its own traditions, and its own religious practices (or *non*practices, as the case may be), but in one way all families are alike, and that—as I noted earlier—is in the way we tend to pass our flaws on from one generation to the next. I only repeat this because it's worth repeating: This is a mistake you should work hard to erase.

> ❧
>
> THE CHILD WHO KNOWS HIMSELF—BE IT THROUGH ROUTINE, TRADITION, OR FAITH—IS STRENGTHENED BY THAT SELF-KNOWLEDGE.
>
> ❧

I often tell my kids: "Divorce often begets divorce. Violence certainly begets violence. And a man who was raised by emotionally distant parents runs the risk of becoming a distant parent himself, in large part because he knows nothing else. But we are responsible for our own actions. We can look to our personal history to try to figure out why we turned out the way we turned out, but we can't use that history to condone bad behavior. If a man was yelled at as a child, it doesn't give him the right to yell at his children.

"I want this family to be the healthiest family it can be. That is why we have these conversations. So we can talk about everything."

Parents come to me and tell me that their children don't want to talk, that they're sullen and curt and monosyllabic. And I tell them, "That's just not acceptable. No matter what mistakes you may have made in the past, your children need to know that *you are a family*. This is not negotiable. Inspire them to answer and share."

Not long ago a woman came to see me about her fifteen-year-old daughter. "She wants nothing to do with me," she said. "I've done nothing wrong, but she does everything in her power to avoid me and shut me out of her life.

> ∽
> DON'T MAKE
> DYSFUNCTION A
> FAMILY TRADITION.
> ∽

When I try to talk to my friends about this, they all say the same thing: 'It's okay. That's what they do at fifteen.' But I can't take it. I feel so unappreciated. I do *everything* for her, and all I want is a relationship with her, but she won't even look me in the eye. I only found out she had a boyfriend because one of my own friends told me about it. Do you have any idea how humiliating that was?!"

As I see it, there are basically two ways of dealing with this problem. The first is through guilt: "I slave all day waiting tables so you can eat! It would be nice if you showed a little appreciation from time to time!" That doesn't work. A parent must never be put in the position of a supplicant. And even if the child softens, it's only temporary. Besides, do you really want to elicit *pity* from your children? The second way, the right way, is through inspiration, and that comes down to reinforcing the inescapable fact that *you will always be a family*, regardless of how your child happens to feel about the subject.

Let me give you an example. There was a man on our television show who had been adopted at a very early age and, for a number of reasons, had never felt sufficiently loved by his adoptive parents. I encouraged him to confront his father about his true feelings, and he did so with great respect. "In life, you only get one father," he told him. "You're my one and only father. That will never change. So you and I are going to have to learn to be closer. We have no choice. You can't choose another son and I can't choose another father. This is it. Let's make it work for both of us." They aren't there yet, but they are both working on it, and true progress has been made.

I tell my kids, "I am your father, and you must never forget that. I have made my share of mistakes, but I have always tried to do the right thing. And it's all because I love you and want to be connected to you. I cannot tolerate any distance between us. I never want to be shut out from your life. In everything I've ever done for you, there is only one thing I have ever wanted in return: *for me to be in your life, and for you to be in mine.* And I have the right to expect that. That's what being a family is.

"Other parents will say it's a rite of passage—that kids rebel, that they don't want to be close anymore—and that's fine. *For them.* But that's not *this* parent. Everything we have ever done in this family is designed to bring us closer together. That's been the priority, and it's something I will not negotiate. You will have a close relationship to your family."

You might not get though to them that night, or the following week, or even three months from now, but you will get through to them.

As Bishop Desmond Tutu noted, "You don't choose your family. They are God's gift to you, as you are to them."

And always remember: *Words that emanate from the heart penetrate the heart.*

8

LOVE

LOVE IS THE FORCE IN THE UNIVERSE THAT
BRINGS EVERYTHING TOGETHER; HATE DRIVES
EVERYTHING APART. LOVE IS THE GRAVITY
THAT UNITES US; HATE THE ANTIGRAVITY
THAT RIPS US ASUNDER.

When I was eight years old, my parents divorced, and my mother moved us from Los Angeles to Miami, where she could be closer to her own family. I was devastated by my family's breakup and by the fact that my father was suddenly so far away. I would speak to him on the phone about once a week, and I would see him two or three times a year, mostly on Jewish holidays, when he flew to Miami. I felt distanced from him emotionally and geographically, but I wasn't sure he felt the same way.

Many years later, however, I met a rabbi in Los Angeles, who told me a story about my father.

"After your mother left, he would come to see me every week, and he was a living dead man," the rabbi said. "He would sit and cry all day that his children were so far away from him, that his heart was broken, and that nothing he was doing really mattered anymore. Week after week, for years! I had never seen a man so crushed."

As you might imagine, this was quite shocking to me. My father was a tough, Middle Eastern man, conditioned to show strength above all emotions. Since I wasn't sure he missed me the way I missed him, I held my own feelings in check, and as a result of this misunderstanding we were not as close as we might have been. But when I learned about his true feelings from that rabbi, I made a genuine effort to narrow the distance between us. I realized that my father's tough-mindedness would probably keep him from ever talking about his feelings, but since I now knew what was really in his heart I managed to get past it. Knowing that he loved me made me unafraid to love him back, and over the past few years we have become closer than ever. And my point is this: *You need to show your children what is in your heart.*

YOU NEED TO SHOW YOUR CHILDREN WHAT IS IN YOUR HEART.

I never miss an opportunity to tell my children that I love them, and I often talk to them about the nature of love. I remember reading an article in the *New York Times* about the discovery of something called antigravity, a force of chaos in the universe, and I shared the article with my children. "Gravity keeps everything together, and antigravity creates chaos by tearing everything apart," I told them. "That's a very good metaphor for love and hate. Love is the force in the universe that brings everything together; hate drives everything apart. Love is the gravity that unites us; hate the antigravity that tears us asunder."

I told my kids, "To the best of your ability, you have to increase the gravitational forces that draw people together. You have to ask yourself, 'How can I be closer to other people? How do I show my love?' Even when someone is mean to you, you have to learn to transcend it. Don't become part of the negative forces in the universe because they undermine the very fabric of existence. Don't join the forces of repulsion. Learn to win over the hearts of your enemies. The Talmud says, 'Who is a great man? He who can make his enemies into friends.'"

It is critical to make your kids believe in love, especially if you've been divorced. Children of divorce tend to stop believing. They think they will wake up one morning and the sun won't shine, or that the flowers won't bloom in the spring. They are seriously rattled by divorce, because the two people whose union was responsible for their very existence have gone their separate ways.

I can almost always tell children of divorce or those from unhappy homes. They are generally more reserved and more cynical than other children, and early on they exhibit signs of hardness. These children begin to suspect that love is a myth. As they grow up, they find it challenging to extend themselves or to be selfless because they haven't seen that type of behavior work in their own homes. Quite the contrary, they've seen it *not* work, and they have no reason to believe it will ever work for them. As they move toward adulthood, they are more likely to operate in a harsher reality. They believe that nice guys finish last, that no good deed goes unpunished, and that people are only altruistic when it suits them. A child without love feels abandoned and lost and very much alone in the world.

When I see those types of kids, it fills me with pain, and unfortunately I am seeing more and more of them every day. My children see them, too— they go to school with them, live across the street from them, socialize with them—and as a result we often find ourselves talking about the very nature of love. "Love is like karma," I tell my kids. "What goes around comes around. Let me paraphrase from King Solomon: *All relationships are like looking into a reflective pond. What you show others is what will be reflected back to you.* If you show people love, it will be reciprocated. That is an axiomatic law of the universe: Love works."

Part of believing in love is believing that there's a common origin to all of humanity; and since we all come from the same place and are made of the same "stuff," we can always find something in another person to relate to. "People want to love, people want to share love, people want to be close—that's part of human nature. When they behave in a mean-spirited fashion, they're being untrue to themselves. All we need to do is to remind them of their truer self. It goes back to what we always talk about in this house: *listening to that inner voice.*

"If you're hurt, and especially if you're hurt in love, you will condition yourself to ignore that voice, and you will stop believing, and I never want you to stop believing."

A child who believes in love, who feels your love, knows that he will never be alone in the world.

Let me tell you a story that illustrates what I mean: A few summers ago, our three older kids went to sleepaway camp in the Catskills, and my wife Debbie took the younger kids to Australia to visit her parents. I was alone at home, working on my radio show, and at the end of two weeks I went to the Catskills for Visitor's Day. I got up early in the morning and was the first parent there. When my daughters saw me, they were so excited that they ran over and smothered me with hugs and kisses. It was a very special moment: Their mother was ten thousand miles away, they had been without family for two whole weeks, and in that moment of complete openness they held nothing back.

> ❧
>
> A CHILD WHO BELIEVES IN LOVE, WHO FEELS YOUR LOVE, KNOWS THAT HE WILL NEVER BE ALONE IN THE WORLD.
>
> ❧

We had a wonderful day. I had brought Chana's little Maltese dog with me, and we went hiking and canoeing on the Delaware River, and then we had an early dinner and made our way back to camp. As we pulled into the parking lot, the girls became very emotional. Chana, who was eleven at the time, was holding her little dog as if her life depended on it. With tears streaming down her cheeks, she quietly asked me not to leave. It was really one of the saddest things I had ever seen. I took her aside and said, "Wherever I go, wherever you go, I'm always with you because my children are always the number one thing in my heart and mind. You guys are the center of my existence. My radar is on you at all times. You can always feel my love and my presence. I don't go anywhere without you. You are always with me. You're in camp because it's a good experience for you, but your father is still with you. You never have to feel alone. There is nothing in my life and in the life of your mother that comes before you."

> I WILL KEEP TELLING THEM I LOVE THEM, EVEN IF THEY THINK I'M BEING SCHMALTZY, BECAUSE I DO LOVE THEM AND I WANT THEM TO KNOW IT ALWAYS.

Those words comforted her (more or less!). I had to pry her hands loose from the dog, but she eventually stopped crying, kissed me goodbye, and went back to camp.

Of course, things don't always work out quite that smoothly. Sometimes I will speak to my kids from the bottom of my heart, and I can see that I'm not reaching them. They might smirk and roll their eyes. But I just keep going. I don't accept it.

I refuse to let it affect me. I will keep telling them I love them, even if they think I'm being schmaltzy, because I do love them and I want them to know it always.

Still, kids are going to push you away, particularly as they get older. They are trying to cut the umbilical cord, trying to assert their independence, and that's fine, but you can't let it stop you. You have to remind your children, constantly and tirelessly, that you love them. And you have to do so especially at those moments when they are determined to test your love. They need to know you love them even if they don't want to hear it, and even *especially* when they don't want to hear it. They may scoff and try to reject you. They'll tell you that you're embarrassing them. They'll tell you to leave them alone. But you must never stop showing them how much you love them; to do otherwise is to capitulate to their evolving cynicism.

I tell my kids, "I know sometimes you are embarrassed by the way I show my love for you. Well, tough. Too bad. You'll just have to live with it. I am never going to mask my affection for you. Ever. You are my children, and I will never be ashamed that I love you. I will not hold back, so you have no choice but to get used to it."

Kids might want to show you that they don't need the mushy stuff, but don't let them fool you: We all need it.

From time to time, one of my children might appear troubled or remote, and I don't let it slide, no matter how busy I am. "What is it?" I ask. "Why do you look so upset? Tell me what's bothering you." Sometimes I'll take the opposite tack: I might approach one of my children when he or she is in an unusually *good* mood. "Do you know that a moment like this—seeing you smile, seeing you happy—is more precious to me than anything in the world. These are the moments I live for, these are the moments that bring me infinite joy."

Often, when we're gathered together, I'll just tell my kids what's in my heart—and I don't need a reason to do it: "You kids sustain me. Do you know that? When I'm away from you, I can't ever be happy. But when I come home and see your faces, I'm comforted and happy."

They might smirk or giggle, and they might think I'm being a silly sentimentalist, but I say it anyway, because I know from experience that I'm getting through to them—that these words stay in their hearts.

While you can *spoil* your child, you can never *love* your child too much. The love you share with your child remains stored in his heart. And it will help him through the dark patches ahead.

Children are not likely to remember all the things you gave them, but they will always remember the love you poured into their lives.

9

Fεar

A CHILD WHO MεASURεS HIS SεLF-WORTH
THROUGH GRADεS, POPULARITY, AND εVεN
HIS POSITION ON THε LITTLε LεAGUε TεAM
WILL CARRY THAT INTO ADULTHOOD, AND
HIS εNTIRε LIFε WILL Bε COLORεD BY
SKεWεD, FεAR-DRIVεN VALUεS.

"Of all base passions, fear is the most accursed." Shakespeare uttered those immortal words, and I couldn't agree more. There are few emotions that exert the debilitating influence of fear, yet children today seem to live in constant fear—so much so that fear seems to be a congenital condition for them. They are afraid of family discord. They are afraid of not being beautiful enough, handsome enough, or popular enough. They are afraid of poor grades, afraid of not being picked for the team, and even, in some cases, afraid of life itself.

To compound matters, we *teach* our children to be afraid: of strangers, of the unknown, of the future. And we make them afraid by example: "An F! My God, aren't you ashamed of yourself!" Well, I hope not. To be *afraid* of an F is far worse than the grade itself: It teaches the child to fear failure.

A parent's job is to help the child confront his fears, whatever they may be, not to reinforce them through word and deed. When you threaten a child for questionable behavior, for example, you are teaching him to fear your wrath, and if he addresses the behavior at all it is only because he fears the consequences. On the other hand, when you discuss that behavior, *without threats*, you are conditioning him to address it in an environment that is free of menace. He will find his way because you helped him find his way, not because he was terrorized into doing so.

The goal of these conversations is to inspire the child understand his fears, and thereby to master them. Fear robs us of vitality and humanity. Children who live in fear become less adventurous, less truthful, less *alive*. Fear is like a dark cloud that blocks out the sunlight. The goal is to live fearlessly, with caution, not to live with so much caution that you live in fear. Fear is a hysterical response to an imagined threat; caution is a calculated response to a real danger.

You might say, "But I *want* my child to be afraid of that creepy guy in the raincoat, lurking by the school yard!" And I'll say, "You're wrong. You want your child to be *cautious* enough to know that he needs to look out for that creepy guy in the raincoat, not to fear him.

> ❧
>
> FEAR IS A HYSTERICAL RESPONSE TO AN IMAGINED THREAT; CAUTION IS A CALCULATED RESPONSE TO A REAL DANGER.
>
> ❧

If he fears him, he will be afraid to act if anything happens. If he doesn't fear him, he will speak out and make himself heard."

I tell my kids, "You can never allow a fear to conquer you, because you're bigger than any fear, you're stronger, truly indomitable—nothing can defeat you in life. The only time anything can defeat you is if you become afraid of it."

Often a child will come to you with a fear that seems unimportant, and the temptation is to dismiss it out of hand. But what the child is really telling you is that *he feels alone*. Fear speaks to existential angst, even if the child is unaware of it. He wants to know that the world makes sense, that he has some power, that he is not as alone as he feels, and to dismiss his fear as unfounded is unhelpful in the extreme.

When my son Mendy came home that day to tell me that the other boys didn't want to play football with him, we talked about it at length because I knew how *alone* it made him feel. It later became the basis of a dinner table conversation about popularity, and about the pitfalls of giving other people the key to your self-esteem. "You must never let someone else decide whether you have value as a person," I told my kids. "Only *you* have the power to make yourself feel better about yourself. If you give someone the power to make you feel good, you're giving them the power to make you feel bad, too. If they invite you to their house for the weekend, you're happy. If they don't, you're sad. Why should they have that kind of power over you? In your zeal to be liked, to be popular, you are looking to them for approval. And while all of us want to be liked, we have to ask ourselves, *At what price?*"

Grades, popular opinion, style, fashion, looks—all of these can turn into sources of fear, if we let them. *A child must learn to be the arbiter of his own value.* To let others judge us is to live in fear, and to live in fear is to become diminished. Fear makes us recoil from the world. Fear begets fear and gives rise to new and ever-stronger fears.

One of my favorite fear stories concerns George Washington's crossing of the Delaware River on Christmas Eve, 1776. I often share that incredible story with my kids: "Here was a man who had been humiliated in battle. In the space of a few months, his troops had been reduced to a ragtag army of defeated men chased out of New York, many of them stumbling around with no shoes. People were saying that Washington was the worst general ever, that he was afraid and incompetent, and had he listened to them he might have come to believe that he really *was* incompetent, that he really *was* afraid. But he decided not to listen. He listened to his own inner voice. Instead of listening to other people—*Love the jacket!/Your hairstyle is way cool!/You're really brave, dude!*—he listened to himself, the one person who really counted, and he devised the most daring plan of his military career. He took his utterly demoralized soldiers, most of whom were starving

> ↬
> A CHILD MUST LEARN TO
> BE THE ARBITER OF HIS
> OWN VALUE.
> ↬

and woefully underdressed, and on Christmas Eve, 1776, a bitterly cold night, led them across the frozen river in unstable boats and attacked the British forces in Trenton."

The story of Washington's crossing is a truly incredible story, and it's really the only reason we're Americans today. That was the single most important victory in the Revolutionary War. The colonists had lost hope. But George Washington was fearless—he refused to let himself be defined by anyone else.

I always remind my children: "Despite everything Washington had suffered, despite every setback, despite everything people said about him, he still wasn't afraid, he still didn't believe the British were stronger than he was. He still believed in his ability to stand up and fight. And it was his faith in himself, and in his personal leadership, and in the righteousness of his cause, that changed the course of history. *Not what other people said; not what other people told him to think or feel about himself; not the things he was expected to be afraid of.* No. Not at all. The reason America is a country today is due to the invincibility and fearlessness of one man. One man. One action. One night. It came down to that."

Children don't fight battles, of course, but on a daily basis they struggle with skirmishes of their own. For example, all young girls go through phases of feeling plain and unattractive, and, as girls, they feel instinctively that they are being judged first and foremost for their beauty. You can't ignore this seminal, contemporary fear. You have to confront it head on.

Tell them, "When you believe you're beautiful, you *are* beautiful. When you believe you're attractive, you *become* attractive. Not in some shallow way, but in the deepest possible way. The whole of you is attractive: your character, your personality, your looks. It all melds into one powerful package. And I'm telling you that you *are* beautiful. I know you think I'm biased because I'm your father, but you're wrong. I know you better than anyone in the world—I know you inside and out. And you are genuinely beautiful."

I have often told my kids about Cyrano de Bergerac, a truly beautiful man with a big nose. His problem was not that he was ugly, but that he *thought* he was ugly, so he behaved as such, and as a result he was afraid to speak to Roxanne. He believed he was unattractive, and he never allowed himself to see that he was beautiful in ways that were much larger than his nose. That fear colored his entire life.

I tell my children, "Whatever you're afraid of, whatever you *think* you're afraid of, you need to know that you are bigger and more powerful than this thing. To believe otherwise is to let fear through the door."

In my opinion, most of our fears are rooted in the feeling that *we don't really matter.* A child is unable to express this, of course, but that doesn't mean he doesn't feel it. A child can be overwhelmed by the oppressive vastness of the universe and by a sense of his own insignificance, even if he can't put that feeling into words. For him, the feeling usually manifests itself as a terrible loneliness: *Nobody cares about me. I'm alone in the world. If anything happened to me, life would go on and no one would even miss me.*

This fear—that our lives count for nothing—is not the exclusive domain of children. We carry the feeling into adulthood, and it becomes increasingly complex. Nothing is ever enough—cars, houses, money—but we continue to use those things to measure our value as human beings. That is why it is so important to address a child's fears, because this is the time to effect changes. Never let your child feel that his grade, or his position on the team, determines his value—it feeds his fear. Tell him, "Good or bad grades no more determine your value as a person than the cool kid who thinks he is the arbiter of popularity." The fear of not measuring up only exacerbates the feeling that we don't really matter, especially if we peg it to things like academics or athletic performance.

"As Rabbi Yitz Greenberg once noted, every human being is born with three inherent virtues," I tell my children. "One, uniqueness: There's no one on earth like you, which makes you profoundly worthy. Two, equality: No one is better than you; we are all equally God's children. And three, infinite value: Every human being is of incalculable worth—and that goes double for you guys."

A child's fear of insignificance is understandable—the world is a scary, uncertain place—but we mustn't let it take root. Fear renders us inanimate. It freezes us into inaction. It strips us of our dignity. Like the nose on Cyrano's face, it has the power to stop us in our tracks. That is why fear—all fear—must be addressed. A child who measures his self-worth through grades, popularity, and even his position on the Little League team will carry those skewed values into adulthood, and his entire life will be colored by the fear that he doesn't matter. Nothing will ever be enough because he measures himself through the fear-driven values he learned as a child.

As far as I'm concerned, there is only one *legitimate* fear, and that is the fear of God. If you cross that line, you're crossing the moral threshold— you're flirting with wickedness and inhumanity.

I tell my children, "The only thing you need to fear is that you will betray God's moral code. If you take God's commandments to heart, and you live by those commandments, you have absolutely nothing to be afraid of.

"That is why they're there. To live your life according to the Ten Commandments is to live a life that's free of fear."

10

GOD

THE PLACE OF GOD IN OUR LIFE IS TO
ALWAYS REMIND US OF THE MORAL
QUESTION. GOD DEMANDS RIGHTEOUSNESS.

The first thing I want to do in this chapter is tell you why I think it's *necessary* to talk to kids about God, and why it is essential to a child's upbringing.

First, kids need to know that there's a moral context to the universe—that there's a plan and a design—that life is not capricious or accidental. There's a governor, a regulator, a supervisor—a God who really watches and scrutinizes our actions—*an eye that sees, and an ear that hears,* as the Talmud puts it.

And they need to know this because the greatest destroyer of childhood, and of a child's security, is purposelessness. The feeling that their existence is not meaningful; that nothing matters. Work, people, possessions, relationships, life itself—none of it matters. The culture teaches them as much, and it begins in the home.

> ❧
>
> KIDS NEED TO KNOW THAT THERE'S A MORAL CONTEXT TO THE UNIVERSE—THAT THERE'S A PLAN AND A DESIGN—THAT LIFE IS NOT CAPRICIOUS OR ACCIDENTAL.
>
> ❧

Divorce is just one example. The child whose parents divorce—and, remember, that's about half of the children in America today—thinks that life is a series of accidents. The parents may have had love once, but now it's gone, so it couldn't have meant that much to begin with. *Nothing lasts. It's all expendable, and so am I.*

Materialism is another example: Children see people pouring their lives into ephemeral pursuits. They acquire things that make them feel good (for a minute or two), then move on to the next thing, and the next one after that, and they remain trapped on that consumer treadmill for the rest of their lives.

Man's inhumanity to man is a third example, and the most brutalizing. This is beyond a child's understanding. The universe is fickle. Bad things happen. *I wonder if they'll happen to me?*

Finally, there's death, which is truly incomprehensible to a child. One day you're alive, the next you're gone. *What's the point? Nothing matters. Everything ends.*

When we teach kids about God, however, we are telling them that life is neither purposeless nor meaningless, and that each one of us is part of a divine plan.

Most Americans believe in God, and they believe in their own fashion. Nearly 80 percent of Americans, for example, don't believe in evolution. Some 50 percent dismiss it out of hand, and the other 30 percent say they believe in evolution by virtue of intelligent design. That means that half of them dismiss it as an unsound scientific theory—*Man came from apes! I don't think so, pal!*—and another 30 percent accept it, but only because they believe an intelligent designer (God) used evolution as an agency to bring about creation.

> ❧
>
> THE GREATEST DESTROYER OF CHILDHOOD, AND OF A CHILD'S SECURITY, IS PURPOSELESSNESS.
>
> ❧

On hearing something like this, many people will jump to the conclusion that Americans are simply not very bright, and that they are easily influenced by myth. That is, in fact, the way many liberals in this country see it, and indeed the way most Europeans see it: They think the majority of Americans are uneducated, superstitious, country bumpkins who believe in fairy tales. But that is neither a fair nor an accurate assessment. Indeed, it is both arrogant and prejudiced.

In his gripping book, *A History of the American People*, British author Paul Johnson argues that this country grew to become a huge superpower primarily because its people had a religious belief about their destiny. Americans were purposeful from the very beginning, he said. It's as if they always knew that they would become a great nation. From their earliest days, they spoke of their *manifest destiny*, referenced the Creator in the Declaration of Independence, and had such faith in God that they put His name on their money and included Him in the Pledge of Allegiance.

That is part of the American mind-set—that things don't happen by accident, that there *is* a master plan—and this is a result not of superstition, and not because Americans lack education, but because they have *an almost visceral reaction to the idea of purposelessness*. And that sense of direction, coupled with a zealous belief in the American

Way of Life, is the reason America is so quick to take its vision of faith, democracy, and government to all corners of the globe, by force if necessary. Because they are True Believers, the American Way is the American religion.

In his book, Johnson points out that some of the most successful American products have been marketed with almost religious zeal. Coca-Cola, for example: *Coca-Cola. It's the Real Thing.* It's almost as if it were being sold as a Higher Truth. Or look at Nike: *Just Do It.* Don't think about it; don't overanalyze it. Do it because it makes sense and because you know it's going to work out. That's *faith.* If you do it, it will happen. If you build it, they will come.

Europeans consider themselves to be more sophisticated than Americans, more educated, more intellectual, and more introspective. But if Johnson's theory is to be believed, they are less successful because they lack faith.

Like it or not, religious zeal is the heart of America, and it works. The vast majority of Americans believe that life has purpose, and that sense of purpose and direction is what keeps them going.

What keeps children going? The same thing. They need to know that life is *not* capricious, *not* accidental, but purposeful and meaningful.

A parent who allows his child to sit in front of the television for five hours a day is sending the wrong message. *Life is meaningless,* he is saying. *Go ahead and burn five hours in front of the tube. In the end, you die. It's all stupid.*

But a parent who teaches his child about God is on the right track. *God is the supreme designer of creation; God has a plan for your life; God gave you unique gifts; God has never created a single person in error.*

That parent is telling his child: *You matter.*

My conversations with my kids about God usually take place just before the youngest ones go to bed, when all the children are in their pajamas, and we sit down to read the Bible together. I'll read some great Biblical story, and I'll try to make them really understand God. I'll say to them, for example, "Look at King David. The Bible says he was a volatile, hot-tempered redhead, but God saw promise in this man. The whole story of David is about God trying to steer him to funnel all of his gifts into doing something life-affirming. God doesn't shy away from King David's volatility. God isn't looking for him to be some goody-two-shoes. God loves David's energy, but He also sees that uncurbed it will lead him down the wrong path. And God is always rebuking David. 'You took someone else's wife!' 'You counted the people as an act of vanity to show how big your dominion was.' And so on. God keeps trying to inspire David to be better.

"Do you see what God was doing? Do you understand what this means?

"The place of God in our life is always to remind us of the moral question. God demands righteousness."

I often say to my children, "Who are the real heroes in our society? I'll tell you: They are the men and women who do the right thing because it's the right thing to do. Even when, and especially when, no one is looking. You don't do it for the reward. You do right because it's right, not for any ulterior purpose.

"I know sometimes you think life is unfair. You do something bad, you get called on it. Then you do something good and nobody notices. But God notices. God knows what you did, good and bad, and you need to remember this always.

"He is watching. He will know if you do something bad. He will probably not do anything about it. But He will know, and *you* will know."

A child needs to be made aware of this. It gives his life meaning. It lends significance to every single action. It *all* matters, from the biggest to the smallest. *To do the right thing because it is right*—that is the essence of the God conversation. That there is always someone watching. That God takes pride in your good actions, and, conversely, is wounded by the bad ones.

I tell my kids, "When you attach yourselves to God, and to Judaism, you are part of an eternal nation—and that makes you unstoppable. Light will always triumph over darkness. You light a tiny candle in a big room and all the darkness is dispelled. One tiny little flame—that's what your life is."

Alas, life, and the explanations for it, are not always without challenges. A little over a year ago, my children's Jewish day school in New Jersey experienced an unspeakable tragedy: A fire claimed the lives of four children in a single household. Two of my kids shared classes with the victims, and they were devastated and stunned, and I understood that only real, deep conversations about the blessings and imperfections of life could fill the void that had developed in their hearts. I did not patronize my kids with stories about what those deaths meant. Rather, I told them the truth—the truth as I saw it, and as I see it to this day.

> ❧
>
> TO DO THE RIGHT THING BECAUSE IT IS RIGHT— THAT IS THE ESSENCE OF THE GOD CONVERSATION.
>
> ❧

This led to one of the most important conversations I've ever had with my children, and it's a conversation that we've never stopped having. A tragedy of that magnitude—four young children, dead, in a fire—makes you question everything. How does one deal with something like that? How does one explain it? And the fact is, the average God conversation doesn't really address it. The parent tells the child that God loves him and will always take care of him and that nothing bad is going to happen. But a bad thing just happened! What they're telling the child doesn't always accord with his experiences. *Look what happened to those poor kids! How can God be so cruel and indifferent?*

I told my kids, "You must always have a real and honest relationship with God, and part of that relationship gives you the right to be angry when He allows bad things to happen. We may not know the answers, and we may never know the answers, but we have a right to object to God's actions *because God Himself expects it.* After all, He commands us to stand up for life, and that applies even when He has taken that life.

"God controls the world," I tell my children. "And we thank Him for all of the good things He does for us. The fact that there's love in the world, that we have food to eat, that our family is together—we're very grateful for all of that. And you know something? In my opinion, life works out almost 99 percent of the time. And we say 'Thank God' for that. But 1 or 2 percent of the time things go horribly wrong. Children die in fires. Children contract leukemia. And mothers and fathers can't put food on the table."

At those moments in our relationship with God, we need to be authentic—we're not going to paper them over. We're not going to suddenly say, "This is God's plan. It's for the best. Those four kids were special souls and God wanted them in heaven." That's patronizing, and an insult to the child's intelligence. It's about as convincing as the Tooth Fairy.

I tell my kids: "You have a right to be angry at God, because your relationship with God is real. This is a tragic event, and it is devastating. You have to cry out to Him, 'God, how could you allow something like this? I pray to you every day, God. I believe in your goodness. In all my prayers, I've been taught that you are life-affirming and gentle and long-suffering. Where were all those qualities in evidence when these children burned alive? I want to have a real relationship with you, God, and I'm asking you to *stop* these tragedies. You're God! You're capable of it! And I'm not looking for explanations. 'The children died for this reason or that reason.' I just want the world to be a better place. That's what I pray for. I don't seek to *understand* bad things. I just don't want them to ever happen again. That's what I invoke from you. That's what I *demand* of you.'"

Children have to be taught that they have a right to make those demands. When my children come to me to complain about my own shortcomings, they don't want to hear that I yell at them because I had a turbulent childhood. That's just a poor excuse! They don't want an explanation. They want to have a stable and peaceful family life, which is what they deserve as children. *And that's what they deserve from God as well.* What would be the point of having a relationship with God if it was a dishonest relationship? If you can't tell God what's in your heart, if you can't show anger and frustration, you're not being true to yourself or to your relationship with Him—and surely that's not what He wants.

For all the strength and beauty of Christianity, this is one aspect of it with which I have always been at odds. Why isn't one permitted to challenge God? Why must one assume that God is always right and that there must be a good, cosmic reason for children to die in fires?

Similarly with Islam. The word *Islam* literally translates as *submission*, to submit. "God is always right. God is great."

Judaism takes a markedly different approach. The word *Israel* translates, literally, into *He who wrestles with God*. I teach my kids all the time to wrestle with God. We Jews have had a three-and-a-half-thousand year relationship with God, which has also incorporated a three millennia struggle and debate with God. We thank Him for the good times, but we also hold Him accountable for the bad. That's what makes Judaism unique: We give humanity a unique role in the Divine Plan. We are not cosmic chaff. We have a right to demand justice from God. That's why Abraham was the first Jew, because he pleaded with God not to destroy Sodom and Gomorrah. He said to God, "You're wrong! You're the judge of the earth, how could you not practice justice?" These are amazing things for a man to say to God—to accuse God of seeming injustice. Moses did the same thing. God wanted to destroy the Jewish people over the golden calf, and Moses said to God, "You want to destroy the people for being idolaters? After bringing them out of Egypt, splitting the sea, and the ten plagues? Go ahead and destroy them if that's what you want, but take my name out of the Torah. I would rather have nothing to do with your holy Torah if you're the kind of God that would allow so many people to suffer. If you have some cosmic reason to kill people and destroy entire communities that is beyond my own puny, mortal comprehension, that's fine. Go ahead and do what you have to do. But keep me out of it—that's not where I'm at." And how was it resolved? God relented and let the people live. The same thing happened with Abraham. God gave in to his plea to spare the city so long as it contained ten righteous inhabitants.

I tell my kids, "You're allowed to be angry at God. You're allowed to make demands. It is through you, God's children, that God's will is realized. Without humanity, God cannot be known on earth. We reveal Him. By talking to God honestly, you are making yourself count, you are making a difference."

And that's the concept—an amazing, theological concept. The Jews sincerely believe that God wants and expects us to clamor for justice, that He wants us to hold Him accountable when others suffer.

"At the end of the day, we don't know why God lets terrible things happen, and maybe we shouldn't be asking the question," I tell my kids. "If a child dies of leukemia, we can say it was the will of God, the child was an angel—all that meaningless talk that comforts no one. Or we can push God for an answer: 'No, God! It's not okay! I want to *know!* How could you let this happen?' And let's imagine for a moment that God actually comes to you with an explanation: 'He had to die because of X, Y, and Z, and it was all part of the Big Plan.' Now you have your answer, but are you satisfied? You might say, 'That was a good explanation, God, and I think I get it, more or less, but you're God, for God's sake. Couldn't you have done it in some other way, where nobody suffered, where no parents have to grieve over their children's coffins?'"

I say to my kids: "That's the reason we don't ask for an explanation. We don't want to know 'why.' We don't want to know what the plan was. We don't want to know why there was a Holocaust—we want there to *not have been* a Holocaust. Similarly, no child should die of leukemia. No matter how good the reason, and no matter how well God explains it, it is still a terrible, heart-wrenching thing.

"We don't look for answers because the answers will not satisfy us, but we can get mad at God because through our anger we are pushing Him to do things differently next time; we are making ourselves heard. And you know what? That's our job. To make God listen to us."

I often tell my children about Rabbi Levi Yitzhak, a great rabbi from the city of Berditchev, in Russia. He was famous for sparring with God;

he was known throughout the world as a guy who constantly argued with God. It shocked people because he was such a saintly man, and clearly God loved him for it. And I tell my children the story that once, on Yom Kippur, the holy night, the night of atonement, thousands of people came to pray with him, as always. It was standing room only. And he got up and said, "I want to have a conversation with God tonight. Right now." And in front of all those people, he plunged in: "Listen, God, we're all here to ask for atonement for our sins," he said. "If we have desecrated the Sabbath, if we lied, if we stole a little bit—we're sorry. But you know what, God? As I sit here asking for that, I recall now that not one of us turned a woman into a widow this year—but you did, God; not one of us made children orphans this year—but you did, God; not one of us gave a fatal disease to anyone this year—but you did, God. It seems to me that *you* should be asking *us* for forgiveness. But I'll tell you what, God. I'll make a deal with you. You forgive my community, my congregation, the flock of Israel, for the *little* bad things they did, and we'll forgive you for the horrendous things you allowed. Do that for me and we'll call it even."

That's an honest relationship with God. Here was a rabbi who had so much faith in God that he believed that everything happened as a result of Divine Will. *Everything.* That's a lot of faith.

"When he challenged God," I tell my children, "he was actually asserting the greatest testimonial of faith. He believed in God so much that he knew God was capable of stopping all this stuff. That's why he challenged him. It isn't a challenge to *faith.* On the contrary, it's what faith is ultimately all about. It suddenly makes God real to people, because the relationship is honest and we get to retain our human feelings."

Unfortunately, so much of religion today is about suppressing our emotions toward God. Children are not allowed to feel human around God, not allowed to feel anger, not allowed to feel disappointment, not allowed to question Him. Well, what is that? We are promoting a fake relationship, and that's why God has become so impotent in people's lives.

When my kids and their friends learned about that terrible fire, an unspeakably traumatic experience—four kids from their school, four kids from one household, *dead*—they were absolutely devastated. And the school invited several rabbis to the school to talk to the children about it, to try to comfort them. One by one the rabbis stood in front of the children and said the same thing:

They're with God. They're better off. This was His plan. He will take care of them. And the kids hated those speeches. My kids, all the kids. And my kids went around telling anyone who would listen: "No! That's wrong! God should never have allowed this!" And their attitude scandalized a great many people, including some of the teachers, who said I was wrong for teaching such things to my children. Some even called me a heretic! But here's the thing: My kids were able to deal with the tragedy with their relationship with God intact and even strengthened, and they were able to do this because they were able to express their anger and their outrage. As a result, their faith in God *increased*. Because they understood that if they were going to have a relationship with God, it had to be authentic. They had a right, and even an *obligation*, to spar and wrestle with God.

It wasn't their job to exonerate God. It was their job to express their true feelings, based on the values that God told them to hold dear, and if they were shocked and disappointed with what had happened, they had a right to tell Him so. Then they could go back to keeping all of God's commandments. Their objections to God did not sever their relationship with Him, but reinforced it. That is what an honest relationship with God comes down to: truthfulness, honesty, speaking from the heart. It all goes back to that inner voice, call it what you will: *Conscience, Soul, Spirit, Innermost Will, Deepest Self, Quintessence.* It is all about getting in touch with the Pure You. And perhaps, at the end of the day, that's where God resides.

For me, one of the most powerful verses in the Bible comes at the very end, with the death of Moses. He is blessing the people on the last day of his life, at the age of one hundred and twenty, and he goes off to die *alone.*

I tell my children, "The power of this story is this: Here you have the greatest Jewish prophet of all time, the man who with the Ten Commandments brought the great moral code to the world, the man who brought the mighty civilization of Egypt to its knees, truly a great man—and look at how he dies. He ascends the mountain, forlorn, abandoned, and no one is even allowed to go up with him to comfort him in his last moments. And there he dies, completely isolated, with almost all of his dreams broken. He wasn't allowed to go into the Promised Land. He died in Jordan, not in Israel, and it fell to his student, Joshua, to lead the people into Israel. There would be no one there to mourn him, no statue erected to his glory, no twenty-one-gun salute.

"He exits the world's stage quietly, and he is gone. And the point is this: It was never about glory; it was never about a reward; it was never about being remembered. He had done the right because it was right. And that's the thing: *It was never about him; it was about God.*

"And that's why the Bible ends with that incredible story, the ultimate high note of sacrifice and humility, to teach us that that's the way to live. You do it for God. You do it because it's right. You do it for morality, for justice, for goodness, for righteousness, even if you have to suffer for it. Even if all the good you did was never known or was instantly forgotten.

"I repeat: God knows everything. And it's enough that He knows. But it's good that you know, too.

"And as you go through life, you must try to guide your actions by one thing and one thing only: Would God, the supreme moral authority, the supreme governor of the universe—would He approve of my actions? Would He want me to do what I'm doing or not?"

And the interesting thing is, if you can teach your kids to try to live this way, it will teach them *to look deeper.* If they can learn to look beyond the surface, if they can peer beneath the hood, the world will reveal itself to them in all its majesty.

Not only will they understand their own motivations, but they'll understand the motivations of others, and they'll be more forgiving, more resilient, more *human*.

The most beautiful things in life can never be seen or touched, like God and love. They are intangible.

Even if you don't believe in God—whether you're an agnostic and you're not sure, or whether you an atheist and feel certain there is no God—you still want to convey to your children that there is a moral order to the universe, that there is a higher authority to which they will have to answer some day. And that doesn't have to mean God. It could mean answering to your own moral conscience (that inner voice). It could mean answering to the community's collective conscience. It could mean answering to the needs of humanity. Whatever it is, we have to convey to our kids that there really is a moral order to the universe, whether human or cosmic, and that it *demands* goodness from each and every one of us.

An atheist desires also, of course, to convey to his child that his existence is purposeful and meaningful. He tells his child that his life has meaning, that he wasn't born by accident, and that his behavior has consequences for himself, for his community, and for his family. An atheist also tells his child, "If people are bullying a kid, don't join in. On the contrary, you should stand up for that kid." And he doesn't do this because he thinks God will frown on his child's behavior, but because he, too, is on the side of righteousness; he, too, accepts the moral code.

There will always be people who don't believe in God, just as those who believe will seldom agree on the details. As a rabbi, for example, I sometimes engage in debate with leading Christian thinkers. And among the differences between Judaism and Christianity is the issue of perfection. The perfection of Christianity lies in just that—perfection. Jesus is portrayed in the New Testament as perfect. He never sins. He never does anything wrong. He doesn't lust. He doesn't yell at his mother. He suffers for other people's sins but has none of his own. He's the perfect man. In fact, he's so perfect that he's divine.

The Christian conception of goodness, then, is that Jesus had no evil in him. To this, the Jew would respectfully respond: *What do I have in common with him? How could I ever be inspired by someone who cannot understand my struggle? I'm a collection of flaws, forever trying to fix myself, and he's perfect! Jesus had no inclination toward selfishness, or to wickedness, so what's the big deal? There's no struggle going on within him. If you're perfect, there's no temptation, and you're never faced with any choices: You always do the right thing.*

The Hebrew view is all about *im*perfection. Moses is flawed—he can't go to the Promised Land because he has let God down by not sanctifying His holy name before the people. Abraham is flawed and parents Ishmael imperfectly. David is flawed and lusts after another man's wife. So why are these men giants? Why are they Biblical figures if they're so flawed? And the answer is this: *Perfection does not lie in never doing anything wrong; perfection lies in the struggle to do the right thing amidst the predilection to do otherwise.*

These were men who always cared about God's word and struggled to honor it, even though the human tendency is to do what *we* want to do. And that's what made them good, moral men.

I tell my children, "The man who struggles is a real hero. The man who fights to do the right thing, that's a true hero. I am not asking you to be perfect, because I am not perfect, and perfection is elusive. All I'm asking is that you struggle, that you fight to become better, that you care enough to maximize your fullest potential. That's all. Be the best person you can be.

Now, really, when you think about it, that's not very hard, is it? The best you can be is not going to be perfect, but it's good enough for me, and it's good enough for God."

The story is told of the Rabbi Zusya of Anipoli, who began to cry as he lay on his deathbed. Many of his devoted students were gathered around him, and they asked him what had brought forth his tears. "I'm afraid of what I'll tell God when I meet him," he answered. "You see, when God asks me, 'Zusya, why weren't you as great as Abraham?' I'll answer, 'Lord, you did not make me Abraham,' And when God asks, 'Then why weren't you as great as Moses?' I'll answer, 'Lord, you did not make me Moses.' But when He asks me, 'Zusya, why weren't you as great as Zusya could have been?' I will have nothing to answer."

God gives us a sense of purpose. God tells us that the world has a design and a plan. God's existence tells the child that his own existence is meaningful.

The principal thing about God, however, especially for kids, is that God is a comforter. God is always there. A child is never alone. God is with him at all times.

By losing ourselves in God, we discover our truest, deepest self.

By letting God into our lives, we are linking to the infinite. And by linking to the infinite, we inspire this generation, and all those to come.

Acknowledgments

I wish to thank Judith Regan for the fourth book that I have published with her. Each book has been, I believe, an important moral statement on an issue of great significance, and each could not have been produced without Judith's commitment toward putting out books that make people want to be better.

My wife Debbie is my inspiration, partner, and companion in all things, none more so than parenting. This is her book as much as it is mine.

My father and my mother sacrificed a great deal for me. I hope that in books like these they will feel that there has been some reward for their labors.

My friend Pablo Fenjves collated the initial conversations that are the soul of this book, edited the material, and finally, lent the amorphous mass structure, without which this book could not have been written. In addition to being an outstanding writer and editor—lucid and profound—Pablo is an even better father, and many of his inspired parenting suggestions found their way into these pages.

Cal Morgan and Laurye Blackford were instrumental in helping this book see the light of day and I am grateful to them as my colleagues for always believing in this project and fighting hard to see it reach fruition.

My children are the reason I wrote this book, and among the various titles I carry, none makes me prouder than parent.

My brothers and sisters are my best friends. We live spread out over the United States and I miss them every minute of the day.

Finally, God Almighty has showered His infinite blessings upon me from the time I was a boy. I pray that my life be a living sanctification of His eternal name.

RABBI SHMULEY BOTEACH
February 2006